VIOLENCE AND THE FAMILY

GILDA BERGER

VIOLENCE

AND THE FAMILY

Franklin Watts ■ *New York* ■ *London* ■ *Toronto* ■ *Sydney* ■ *1990*

Library of Congress Cataloging-in-Publication Data

Berger, Gilda.
Violence and the family / Gilda Berger.
p.   cm.
Includes bibliographical references.
Summary: Examines common trends in sexual and other kinds of abuse
in the family, including wife abuse, child abuse, child sexual
abuse, adolescent sexual abuse, and elder abuse.
ISBN 0-531-10906-2
1. Family violence—United States—Juvenile literature.
[1. Family violence.   2. Child abuse.]   I. Title.
HQ809.3U5B47   1990
362.82'92—dc20   89-27562   CIP   AC

CONTENTS

VIOLENCE AND THE FAMILY

CHAPTER

1

FAMILY VIOLENCE: AN INTRODUCTION

"Home is where the hurt is."
Time magazine,
December 21, 1987

Family violence is a major problem in this country. It exists in staggering proportions and strikes at the very heart of our society. All family members are vulnerable, from infants to grandparents and including adults and children of all ages. The sad fact is that you are more likely to be physically assaulted, beaten, killed, or sexually attacked in your own home at the hands of a loved one than anyplace else or by anyone else. Except for the army in time of war, experts say, the family is the most violent institution in American society!

Although it has always been present, the problem of family violence has only recently been brought into the open. Once thought to be a rare event, violence in the family is now known to be very common and to have extremely harmful effects.

EXTENT OF THE PROBLEM

One of the difficulties in estimating the extent of family violence is in defining the term. Clearly, family violence includes the death or serious injury of one family member caused by another. But, for example, is parental spanking an act of discipline, or is it child abuse? Is a husband who sexually abuses his wife just mean and nasty, or is he guilty of committing a crime?

Generally speaking, family violence includes any acts (from a pinch or slap to murder) carried out with the intention of causing physical pain or injury to another person. Usually the offender is not a stranger but someone the victim trusts and even loves.

At best, national statistics give only incomplete estimates of the incidence and extent of family violence. The National Crime Survey (NCS), sponsored by the federal Department of Justice, collected information on crime victims based on a survey conducted in 60,000 households throughout the United States. This survey, however, reflects only those forms of abuse that victims are willing to label as criminal and report to interviewers.

Also, the Federal Bureau of Investigation (FBI) collects data based on crimes reported to the police. Data on offenses are limited to eight crimes: homicide, rape, robbery, aggravated assault, burglary, larceny, motor-vehicle theft, and arson. Crimes that may be family violence, such as nonaggravated assault, are not reported to the FBI. And data about the relationship between the victim and the offender are collected only for the crime of homicide.

Despite their limitations, though, the figures tell us much about family violence. Consider these statistics:

■ *Roughly 20 percent of all murder victims in the United States are related to their assailants. About one-third of these murders are killings of women by their husbands or boyfriends.*[1]

- *Crimes by spouses or ex-spouses make up the majority—57 percent—of all crimes committed by relatives. About a quarter of the victims of attack by their spouses or ex-spouses reported that they had been the victim of at least three similar crimes within the previous six months.[2]*

- *Battering is the single most common cause of injury to women, exceeding muggings, motor-vehicle accidents, and workplace injuries combined! In fact, between 1.8 and 2.9 million women are battered yearly, according to expert estimates.[3]*

- *Absenteeism from work related to assaults on wives and mothers results in economic loss to the country of millions of dollars every year, plus many millions more in medical bills.*

- *Eight percent of the pregnant women in this country are assaulted by their husbands or boyfriends during the pregnancy. Not only do the assaults inflict psychological and physical damage on the mother-to-be; some also injure or kill the fetus.[4]*

- *About 1.5 million children are seriously abused each year by their parent, guardian, or others. In addition to the reported cases of child maltreatment, there may be yet another million unreported cases. Between 2,000 and 5,000 children die annually as a result of their injuries.[5]*

- *Almost as many teens are mistreated as younger children. An estimated 42 percent of abused children are between the ages of twelve and seventeen.[6]*

- *One of the most common forms of adolescent sexual abuse is incest—the act of sexual intercourse between closely related family members. Incest is estimated to occur in 14 percent of all families. Fathers, stepfathers, uncles, and brothers are the most common perpetrators. In some instances, a father will sexually abuse all of his daughters throughout their preadolescent and adolescent years. One observer estimates that there are over 10 million episodes of incest a year, many with severe long-term consequences.[7]*

■ *Estimates of the extent of elder abuse—the abuse of parents and grandparents by children and grandchildren—vary from 500,000 to 1 million victims annually. The House Select Committee on Aging estimates that only one in every six cases is actually reported. One study concluded that one in ten elderly persons living with a family member is abused.*[8]

KEY CHARACTERISTICS
OF FAMILY VIOLENCE

Family violence permeates all levels of our society and all areas of our country. The problem is not unique to any one particular social or economic group or one particular region. Nor is it restricted to any one sex or age group. Victims come from all types of homes, even the very "best" of families. Family violence has shattered the lives of people of all ages, representing every occupation and profession.

Family violence is the only crime in which the victim always knows the identity of the offender. Moreover, a large proportion of family crimes are committed by offenders who do not see their acts as crimes against victims—who do not know they are victims.

Brainwashing usually accompanies family abuse. Children who are severely punished are told that they are bad and uncontrollable and must be disciplined. Abused wives become convinced that they are not fulfilling their obligations and responsibilities to their husbands and children. And sexually abused children are led to believe that their father's attentions are normal signs of affection.

In addition to suffering physical injuries, victims of family violence often end up blaming themselves for the abuse. The typical response of abused women: "I provoked him. . . . I was being a bad wife, mother, and housekeeper." Children might say, "I know I needed that beating to keep me in line." Sexual-abuse victims are likely to think, "I must have been leading him on." And all the victims harbor the hope that the abuse will stop if they act differently.

An extreme sense of guilt, shame, and embarrassment makes the victims of family violence reluctant to seek help. Many cannot believe that others could possibly understand or identify with their humiliation. This increases the feelings of isolation and hopelessness in victims of all kinds of family abuse.

Some victims come to regard violence as a natural part of family relationships. Among the long-term effects that have been observed are depression, suicidal feelings, self-contempt, and an inability to trust others or to develop intimate relationships outside the family.

Fears of further violence, especially fear of reprisal, often makes the victim hesitant to seek help from the criminal justice system. Economic or emotional dependency, promises of change from the abuser, or a fear that the family might separate also contribute to a reluctance to take part in criminal proceedings.

Before family violence can be stopped, several things must happen. Abusers and victims alike must recognize that a crime is involved. They must realize that, when appropriate, the criminal justice system will intervene on the victim's behalf. Also, the public must become aware of the problem and its obligation in combating it.

In addition, the community itself must respond to the criminal justice system. Communities should develop a multidisciplinary team, made up of social service agencies, schools, churches, hospitals, and individual citizens, to handle incidents of family violence, especially cases involving the physical and sexual abuse of children.

Since family violence tends to be repeated and to grow worse with time, early intervention is critical in preventing abuse. The best of all strategies for dealing with family violence is to be sure it never occurs in the first place. And the best way to accomplish that is through knowledge. Everyone must know that family violence is not a private matter. It is a criminal offense. When incidents of violence occur, society must be prepared to see that offenders are prosecuted to the full extent of the law.

CHAPTER

2

CAUSES OF
FAMILY VIOLENCE

■ *A man was brought to trial for the murder of fourteen members of his family. Authorities said his rampage was set off by the belief that he had been slighted by other people.*

■ *A frail eighty-one-year-old 100-pound woman was found dead on the floor of her home, her body covered with cuts and bruises that suggested a severe beating. Her two sisters, with whom she had lived, told police that they had to hit their younger sister to control her.*

■ *A twenty-two-year-old told the jury at his trial that he had killed his girlfriend by stabbing her twenty times and hitting her with a hammer twenty-eight times out of anger because she threatened to break off their relationship. The note he left on her body read "I told you what would happen if you ever went to leave me. Now the payback is done."*

■ *A wife was charged with putting cyanide in drug capsules that killed her husband. The wife had been deeply in debt and plotted the killing to collect the insurance money.*

The reasons why certain people attack members of their own family are varied and complex. As a result, there are many theories that try to explain the causes of family violence. But most experts see the pattern of family violence as being made up of four main components:

Personal factors

Family situation

Society and its structures

Cultural factors.

No single set of factors is independent. Each one impinges on the others.

PERSONAL FACTORS

Individuals who are involved in family violence are generally described as having low self-esteem. Typically, they are immature, overly dependent, and insecure. The hate-filled man works out his frustrations by beating his wife. The frustrated wife lashes out at the children when she becomes particularly angry or resentful. And the rebellious teenager expresses his hostility by beating up his younger brothers or sisters. For the moment, the violence actually gives the abuser a false sense of his own power.

Often, people who use violence to release built-up anger mistakenly believe that hitting is useful. Parents, for example, use force to control their children's behavior. Some beat down their victims to the point where, for a while at least, they will do anything or say anything to please the batterers and avoid further violence. This gives abusers the feeling that they have a measure of control over someone or something in their lives. Being in control, being masters (or so they think) of a situation, increases their self-esteem.

The abuser (most often the father) picks on the victim to make up for a sense of his own powerlessness, especially with regard to the masculine ideals of our society. Child abuse tends to start with a feeling of weakness or lack of success. A head of household, for example, may be financially strained or unemployed. The abuse can be a way of venting anger against a social situation that seems hopeless or desperate.

Most American husbands in spouse killings say that their violence was caused by the wife's infidelity or her intention to separate or seek a divorce. The violence is the husband's attempt to control his wife by whatever means. The wife's actions, meanwhile, are desperate efforts to resist his coercion. Brinkmanship of this kind often leads to tragic consequences.

All family violence is essentially the abuse of power, a situation in which a stronger person takes advantage of someone who is weaker. Often, the husband's physical size and his control over the family's money allow him to abuse his wife or children without suffering any social or economic consequences. Likewise, the parents' control over the family's supply of food, clothing, and housing often makes them feel that they have a right to hit their children. The victims have to accept the pain because they have no money or resources of their own. Most would find it hard to survive away from the family home.

FAMILY SITUATIONS

Family violence is usually directed against the most vulnerable members of the family—children under the age of six. The approval of child beatings and other forms of violence to raise and discipline children is practically universal.

In many families, violence is tolerated because it is considered a necessary part of child rearing. The father or mother believe it is their God-given right and duty to discipline the children. "The Bible instructs parents to whip their children with a rod," some say. Or, "Welts and bruises are a sign that a parent is doing a good job of discipline."

Surveys show that the majority of Americans approve of parental spanking. After yelling and scolding, spanking is still the principal form of punishment in most families with children under thirteen years of age. Parents who spank accept the notion that children are taught acceptable behavior through punishment. What they don't realize is that violence begets violence. Also, children who are frequently spanked tend to become highly resentful and distrustful of authority.

A number of circumstances may lead to child abuse. Among the early factors are a medically abnormal pregnancy, lengthy labor, or an especially difficult delivery. Other significant elements may be an extended separation from the child in the first six months of life or a serious illness of the infant or the mother during the first year. All such difficulties pose threats to the bonding that normally occurs between parents and infants. Disruptions of this kind may interfere with the formation of good parent-child relationships.

Disabilities or patterns of behavior that make children especially difficult to care for are often associated with child abuse. Youngsters with physical handicaps, mental retardation, emotional disturbances, learning difficulties, or other special problems are often the victims of child abuse.

The parents of children with physical disabilities often suffer an added strain on their relationship because of the increased responsibility for care. Consequently, there is an even greater tendency to resort to violence in the face of disabilities. According to one study, nearly 20 percent of children with cerebral palsy seen over a one-year period at a Chicago care center had been abused.[1]

Children in stepparent families are disproportionately often the victims of family violence. Step relationships may lack the deep bonds of affection and caring that usually develop between biological parents and their offspring. Feelings of attachment and devotion are sometimes shallower toward children of former unions, contributing to conflict between husband and wife.[2]

Alcohol is another factor in family violence. Almost half of all couples reporting violence claim that either the abuser, the victim, or both had been drinking at the time of the incident. Alcoholic families, in comparison with nonalcoholic families, show a much higher incidence of:

Physical child abuse—31 percent to 9 percent

Sexual child abuse—19 percent to 5 percent

Spouse abuse—38 percent to 6 percent[3]

Some studies show a particularly close correlation between abuse of alcohol and incest. Research on homicidal offenders also shows a strong association between violence and alcohol. Victims testifying before the Attorney General's Task Force on Family Violence reported that alcohol was present and a contributing factor in the abuse perpetrated in their homes. Other surveys also indicate that alcohol is involved in 50 percent of all fights or assaults in U.S. homes and in 34 percent of the cases of child abuse.[4]

But alcohol is seldom, if ever, the sole cause of domestic violence. If it were, drinking would lead to violence in cultures around the world. It does not. In our own culture, drinking offers people "time out" from the normal rules of behavior. It also provides a perfect excuse for violence.

When drunk, a person can deny responsibility for his or her actions. Such denial is quite common. Also, Americans tend to expect aggressive behavior from those who have been drinking. Many believe that alcohol lowers inhibitions, lessens self-control, and reduces a person's ability to think rationally. Thus, the violence that occurs is taken less seriously than it should be.

Not only does violence erupt because of alcoholism, but women who suffer abuse sometimes become heavy drinkers as a result of their being abused. Alcoholism among women is a growing problem, and the largest precipitating cause is believed to be spouse abuse. The shame, fear, and confusion that follow wife abuse is thought to be a major factor in turning women to alcohol.

Drug use has long been linked to violent behavior in families. But most experts believe that crack is producing more family troubles than ever, including an epidemic of child beatings, rapes, and murders within families.

One recent case involved a drug abuser who had smuggled her seven-year-old grandson out of the hospital. His mother had taken him there because the grandmother's boyfriend had abused him, driving the child to suicidal behavior. The judge who heard the case ordered the grandmother and her boyfriend to stay away from the boy as well as other children in the family. He said that severe crack use had increased the risk level in the household to a deadly degree.

In another case, a mother filed a petition against her teenage daughter. The mother described the girl as an obese crack addict who beat up her parent to get drug money.

SOCIETY AND
ITS STRUCTURES

Most violent families, it has been found, live isolated lives. Some say that the private nature of the modern family is most responsible for abuse and neglect. "When the walls [of separate houses] went up, the hitting started," says one writer.[5] The industrialization, urbanization, and modernization of America had a powerful impact on the family. Living apart from friends and relatives, parents and children felt unconnected and outside the controls of society. They believed that no one cared about the family or was willing to interfere.

Many troubled families attempt to prevent children from forming relationships outside the home. Eighty-one percent of abusive families in one study preferred not to seek help in resolving crises. And 95 percent of severely abusive families had no continuing relationship with anyone outside the family.[6]

Social isolation may be the price we pay for privacy in our society. Such isolation stops the flow of information to and from the family. It deprives members of the benefits that social contacts can bring. The only children that can survive maltreatment in abusive situations are those who have someone else in their lives who accepts them unconditionally and provides a positive role model.

A majority of studies have found that violence is more likely to occur in lower-income or minority households, even though everyone knows that abuse is not confined to the poor or blacks. But the poor, it seems, run a greater risk because of the difficulties that result from poverty. Households where the husband is unemployed or employed part-time generally have the highest rates of violence between spouses. Also, when unemployment strikes, children often become the targets of adult rage and frustration.

The poor and minorities also have the greater risk of being labeled abused. With identical injuries, the son of someone on welfare is more likely to be considered a victim of abuse than the son of a college professor. In the same way, black children are more likely to be considered abused than white children in the same condition. The reason is simple. The middle-class members of the medical profession who report the cases and the court officials who sit in judgment prefer to believe that most violence occurs in families unlike their own.

High levels of stress in some families have been

blamed for patterns of family violence. The stress may be the result of changing roles of husbands and wives. A wife with a higher-paying or more important job may engender resentment in a husband who earns less. Or it may be that the single parent in a one-parent household finds it difficult to be both breadwinner and homemaker.

The increasing number of single-parent households in America has made children the largest poverty group in the nation. Today, children are far more likely to be living in poverty (income of below $11,204 for a family of four) than the population as a whole. More and more children live in conditions characterized by homelessness, long-term unemployment, high crime rate, and drug and alcohol addiction.

There is also overwhelming evidence that witnessing violence in the home may itself contribute to violent behavior. The family exposes individuals to violence and techniques of violence; the family teaches children that it approves of the use of violence.

Of course, even though the chances of a battered child becoming a battering adult are very strong, not all parents who have experienced violence as children use violence against their children. But children who are abused do *tend* to grow up to be abusive. It may be that parents who were physically abused as children were frequently deprived emotionally as well. Consequently, as adults they may suffer from low self-esteem, depression, and feelings of powerlessness. To compensate, they may attack those who are weaker and less powerful than themselves—that is, their own children.

CULTURAL FACTORS

Violence is part of the American culture. In the media, on the streets, in sports, and so on, violence is commonplace. And violence can beget violence.

The depiction of violence on television and in the

movies, in rock-song lyrics, and in some modern fiction may contribute to family violence to some extent and affect how adults and children approach conflict. What children and adults get from the media can be an instructional tool in terms of teaching abusive behavior.

More than ever our culture accepts violence as a way of teaching children discipline. The use of corporal punishment is widespread. Even the courts seem to encourage parents to use strong-arm discipline tactics on children, though the results are often harmful.

Experts say that there is probably some hitting in almost every home at some time. Of course, severe abuse is far less common. Most parents are able to keep minor hitting from escalating into major abuse. But where there is a dangerous combination of factors—personal problems, little interference from society (perhaps due to social isolation), extreme stress, and frustration—hitting and violence may be among the more commonly accepted ways to raise children and control wives.

In the view of some, violence is a continuum, "beginning with slaps, grabs, and spankings and extending up to murder."[7] Permitting so-called normal acts of violence sets the stage for possible escalation to the more harmful and dangerous behaviors.

Parents have been found to be more tolerant of physical fights among their children than between their children and others. In fact, some children are far more violent with their own siblings than with other children.

Violence is the historical norm of family life in America. Abusing husbands say, "Why shouldn't I hit her? She's my wife." This use of force in our society may stem from the belief that children are the property of parents and wives are the property of their husbands—notions that go back to tenth-century English family law.

The assumption of the man as the head of the family has always been part of the law of our country. The origins go as far back as St. Augustine, for example, who described marriage as a relationship in which "women ought to serve their husbands as unto God." A Roman father could decide if his newborn child would live or die. And he could put an adulterous wife to death. A husband could beat his wife with a rod as long as it was no thicker than his thumb, the so-called rule of thumb. In short, any culture that held women and children in lower regard than men permitted such behavior.

In *Intimate Violence: The Causes and Consequences of Abuse in the American Family,* the authors claim that the roots of domestic violence and sex abuse are found in the intrinsic inequality within the family (husbands dominating wives, parents dominating children).[8] The authors hold out hope for a cultural ethic that deems the hitting of children or spouse wrong and inappropriate. This can only happen, they say, when people everywhere succeed in eliminating the kinds of sexism that still prevail in many homes and in the workplace.

CHAPTER

3

HISTORICAL BACKGROUND AND ISSUES

For hundreds of years people were unconcerned about family violence, though the problem surely existed. As we said, violence, aggression, and severe mistreatment of children date from far back in antiquity. Many sources—paleontological findings and literature as different as that of the Bible and Cinderella—furnish evidence of children being abused, abandoned, or even eaten. A brief survey of our own history in America may point up some important sources of domestic violence.

FROM THE TIME OF THE COLONISTS

As early as the seventeenth century, there were "stubborn child laws" that gave Puritan fathers the right to put unruly children to death. American wives were not permitted to own property. Husbands could collect their wives' wages and could punish wives who displeased them. Generally speaking, men considered themselves their wives' and children's superiors and masters.

With industrialization and the growth of big cities, the problems of wives and children, in particular, became greater. The anonymity of urban life and poor working conditions promoted family violence. Reformers sprang up who looked at child abuse and warned that it was a kind of "pollution" that would spoil future generations of Americans and ruin society.

The first social agency devoted to the problems of family violence arose in the 1870s. It was called the Societies for the Prevention of Cruelty to Children. The organization focused at first on child abuse but gradually shifted its attention to family violence. Boston formed the Massachusetts Society for the Prevention of Cruelty to Children soon after, in 1878. Its so-called child protectors roamed the streets looking for children that should have been in school. Those who were improperly dressed, excessively dirty, or peddling were swooped up by the authorities. Agents acted like police officers. They threatened the parents with arrest, or else they tried to gain custody of the children and place them in institutions.

During the early years of the twentieth century a change took place under the growing influence of feminism. The child protectors of the family-violence agencies gave way to child-welfare workers. Between 1910 and 1930 family-violence work became incorporated into professional social work. From then on, control of the problem was left to state regulations.

The Great Depression of the 1930s was a particularly stressful time for families. With widespread poverty, the agencies largely ignored family violence and focused instead on relieving economic hardship. There was a relative decline in child protection until the following decades, the 1940s and 1950s, when "pro-family" values came to dominate social work.

In the early 1960s, child abuse became recognized as a national problem. The change was largely due to the publication of *The Battered Child Syndrome*, a book by sociologist and physician C. Henry Kempe that appeared in 1962. The book drew a lot of attention to child abuse. Kempe shook many readers—lay people and professionals alike—out of their lethargy as he compared child abuse to other diseases as a common killer of children.

The first child-abuse law was passed by California in 1963. Many other states followed with similar legislation. Now every state requires the reporting of cases. The American Medical Association has issued diagnostic and reporting guidelines so that physicians can comply with the laws.

Before the emergence of the women's movement in the late 1960s, it was generally assumed that marriage, especially middle-class marriage, was a peaceful affair in which violence played no part. A popular family journal, the *Journal of Marriage and the Family*, did not include even a single article on domestic violence from 1932 to 1969. But in the 1970s research on abused children brought to light other forms of family abuse. And the women's movement drew attention to the issue of battered wives.

A 1977 book, *Wife Beating: The Silent Crisis*, written by journalists Roger Langley and Richard Levy, reported that 26 million to 30 million women were abused each year. That staggering number is roughly one-half of all married women! The book led to reports of an "epidemic of family violence." Since then, estimates have varied from thousands to millions. And attitudes range from those who say extreme domestic violence is rare to those who believe it is quite prevalent.

Other research also found that women who were battered by their husbands were often also battered by teenage and older children, especially when the women were elderly. Thus, abuse and neglect of older people also began to be reported and discussed.

The first national child-abuse prevention and treatment law was passed by Congress in 1973. The National Center on Child Abuse and Neglect was created in 1974 to learn more about causes and prevention. In 1984 and 1985 there was a burgeoning of interest and self-help groups, and the U.S. Congress, the executive branch of the federal government, and the media all expressed their concern. An amendment was added to the Child Abuse Prevention and Treatment Act in 1984 to fund family-violence prevention and services. Abused elderly persons were made eligible for services under the family-violence amendment.

In September 1984, the Attorney General's Task Force on Family Violence issued its report. The report made recommendations for action by all levels of society and government. It also gave specific suggestions for the law enforcement and criminal justice systems, victim assistance, abuse prevention, and education programs.

As of December 1985, Children's Trust Funds had been created in thirty states to be used for the protection of children. The money comes from surcharges on fees for marriage licenses, birth certificates, divorce decrees, and taxpayer donations. The funds are to be used for parenting education, the prevention of sexual abuse, parent support groups, day-care centers for children at risk of abuse, and home aides for adolescent mothers with newborn babies.

A PRIVATE VERSUS
A PUBLIC MATTER

Acts of violence in the home are perpetrated by family members who believe that what happens in the home is their business. But many others say that domestic violence is not a private matter. It is a problem of wide social concern.

Advocates of abused wives and children claim that family violence has more long lasting effects, particularly on children, than crimes committed by unknown attackers. Children who are abused, or who live in homes where parents are battered, frequently carry similar kinds of violent behavior into adulthood. A great proportion of those who assault both strangers and loved ones are the product of violent households.

This spiral of violence, experts say, can start with suffering from, or even witnessing, any kind of family abuse—by spouse, parent, trusted adult, or one's own child. Such abuse arouses conflicting feelings of fear and loyalty, love and guilt, and an overriding shame—emotions not usually experienced by those who are attacked by strangers.

Family members are torn between a desire to protect and help a loved one and a responsibility to look out for one's own safety or that of others in the household. Friends who hesitate to intrude in "family matters" or "choose sides" leave the victims to face their attacker alone. Home, the one place on earth where people should feel safe and secure, becomes instead a place of fear and danger.

Reporting violence, some feel, carries risks. Even the police show a reluctance to get involved in family "squabbles." Prosecutors and judges, too, often minimize the problem. The victim's complaints and pleadings for protection are ignored. Reporting the abuse may put the victim in a worse position than before. The attacker may well respond with increased anger at the first possible opportunity.

People who believe that what goes on in the home is a public matter say that we should not deny the criminality of family violence. Law enforcement officers, prosecutors, and judges who continue to accept and support the view that a husband who beats his wife or parents who whip their children have the right to do so may be fueling the spread of violence in our land.

MEDIATION VERSUS ARREST

During the 1960s many psychologists and social scientists believed that arrest was not an appropriate course of action in family-violence cases because it escalated the abuse, broke up families, and often caused the abuser to lose his or her job. Mediation was the preferred solution to most family-violence incidents. The so-called mediation model moved the issue of family violence away from law enforcement and into social services.

Today, many feel that this policy, which avoided arrest, was based on incorrect assumptions. In attempting to be completely fair, mediation assumed both parties equally responsible. But abusive relationships are generally one-sided. The abuser is usually physically superior, and the injured victim is afraid of further harm. Thus, mediation often fails to hold the offender accountable. It gives the abuser no incentive to change his or her behavior. Mediation may inadvertently contribute to a dangerous increase of violence.

Those who oppose mediation in family-violence cases hold that even suspicion of abuse within a family is a legal matter—even if it means dissolving a marriage or taking children away from their parents. Maintaining the bonds of family structure should count for little if there is violence in the home. Thus, abused children should be placed in shelters when necessary. Adult offenders should be put in jail, even if it means depriving the family of an income.

In truth, both extremes may be based on misconceptions. One position rests on the belief that family problems can be worked out. It holds that the abused mothers and children rarely get hurt. If the violence becomes too severe, the mother can always take the children and leave, they say.

The other extreme regards even one spanking as a sign of abusive parenting. They think that every fight between married couples leads to a violent beating. In their view, family disruption is preferable to any kind of family violence.

Today, most workers in the field of domestic relations take the so-called middle-ground position. Society should neither ignore serious harm nor rush to intervene without convincing evidence of truly violent behavior. The reactions of those outside the home, many now say, must be guided primarily by the severity of the abusive act, not the relationship between the victim and the abuser. The police should be no slower to respond to domestic disturbances than they are to violence between strangers. Often, the only major distinction between family violence and other criminal acts of violence is the relationship between the victim and the assailant. Criminal justice is inconsistent if violence committed by strangers results in arrest and prosecution, while violence between family members is considered a family squabble, best resolved by the parties themselves, without resort to the legal system.

Just as law enforcement officers do not normally arrest two strangers who have shoved each other, neither should they arrest two family members engaged in similar behavior. But when someone is found to be the victim of a serious assault within the family, the officer is dealing with a crime.

Simple justice, then, becomes the major ground for taking a harder stand toward family violence. The Attorney General's Task Force recommended that the legal system treat assaults within the family as seriously as it would treat the same assault if it occurred between strangers. "An assault is a crime, regardless of the relationship of the parties. The law should not stop at the front door of the family home."[1]

For a long time, police departments discouraged officers from making arrests in so-called family disputes. Officers were advised to try to calm down the parties and refer them to social service agencies in the community. As a result, the police officers were often accused of failing to enforce the law in family matters. Frequently, the penalties did not reflect the severity of the injury or any prior convictions for the same offense. "In one city, police had been called at least once before in 85 percent of spouse-assault and homicide cases. In 50 percent of these cases, the police had responded five times to family-violence incidents prior to the homicide."[2]

Many women's groups and others criticize this approach of treating domestic assaults less seriously than assaults involving strangers. They take issue with those who fail to provide adequate protection to battered women. Assaults against family members are also crimes against the state and the community, they believe. Arrests send a clear signal that abusive behavior is a serious criminal act and will not be condoned or tolerated.

Between 1984 and 1986 a number of events encouraged police departments to adopt a policy of arrest for incidents of domestic violence. Among the most important was the Minneapolis Domestic Violence Experiment, which found that arrest and overnight incarceration were more effective than other actions in reducing domestic violence.

In Oregon there was a 10 percent drop in domestic homicides following the passage of a mandatory arrest law for offenders who violated a court order of protection for the victim.[3] A victim's chance of future assault was nearly two and a half times greater when officers did not make an arrest.

Most defendants in domestic-violence cases are released prior to trial. This makes the victim especially vulnerable. The defendant may try to get back at the victim for having him or her arrested. Or he or she may threaten the victim with more violence if he or she cooperates with prosecution. Due to the pressure, the victim may decide to withdraw the charges.

Today, courts may protect victims by making protection a condition of pretrial release. In many cases, judges will forbid the offender from returning home under penalty of the law. Such actions have the advantage of prosecuting the abuser while allowing the rest of the family to stay intact.

PREVENTING
FAMILY VIOLENCE

Everyone agrees that the family is the cornerstone of the American community and culture. And preserving various traditional values and nurturing children are our nation's greatest strengths and hopes for the future. Therefore, it is essential that public policy promote the health and well-being of the family and protect its values.

Gradually, people are coming to realize that the repercussions of violence extend far beyond the walls of the home. The cost is great not only in terms of human suffering but economically—in law enforcement, legal, medical, mental health, and other social service costs.

The Task Force made the following recommendations for future actions so that victims would no longer have to suffer alone:

Every effort must be made to recognize and understand the problem.

Everyone must admit that family violence is found at every level of our society.

All victims must know that they need not hesitate to seek help.

All of us must always listen with an understanding heart and act in ways that prevent family violence and protect and support its victims.

CHAPTER

WIFE ABUSE

■ *A mechanic described by neighbors as a quiet, peaceful man was charged with attempting to hire a navy commando to kill his estranged wife.*

■ *Baby Tess May was born prematurely. Her grandmother believes it was because the baby's father beat the baby's mother during pregnancy.*

■ *A former Methodist minister was found liable for the nearly fatal choking of his wife. The woman, who was found unconscious on the floor of their garage, has been in a coma ever since.*

■ *Joseph Pikul, a wealthy New York stock analyst, admitted to police that he killed his wife and said that she "deserved it."*

■ *A business executive, quarreling bitterly with his wife, fired a pistol and accidentally wounded his two-year-old daughter, who was in her mother's arms.*

The battered woman, it has been said, lives in a world of terror and her home is her prison. For many years women were too frightened to report incidents of violence from a partner in an intimate relationship. But the situation may be changing. Today, more and more people are reporting incidents of abuse, and new kinds of help are becoming available to victims.

THE PROBLEM

Whatever shape or form the violence takes, wife abuse, in the words of one victim, "is the most confusing and cruel indignation anyone can suffer." Also called domestic violence or battering, wife abuse can be divided into three main categories:

Physical Violence. Any action that causes pain or injury by hitting with fist, stick, strap, or any hard object, pushing, shoving, grabbing, slapping, kicking, biting, or using a knife or a gun. The results of physical violence include broken bones, concussions, permanent brain damage, hearing loss, and miscarriages.

Psychological Violence. Includes threats of bodily harm, forcing the victim to perform degrading or humiliating acts, depriving the individual of money, clothing, transportation, opportunities to interact with family members or relatives or to develop friendships with others, controlling the spouse's sleeping patterns, eating habits, or social relationships.

Sexual Violence. Includes abuse of the genital area or forced sexual relations. According to clinical case reports, official police records, and social surveys, violence and the threat of violence are often a part of forced sex in marriage.

PHYSICAL AND PSYCHOLOGICAL VIOLENCE

Experts vary greatly in the exact meaning they give to the term "wife abuse." Generally speaking, though, wife abuse includes *any* assault, from minor pushes and shoves to severe beatings, that has a high probability of causing relatively serious—that is, more than temporary—pain or injury.

The instances in which wives are forced to do what their husbands want without regard to their own rights, body, or health are very serious, widespread, and frequent. Consider these figures drawn from various sources:

- *At least 1.8 million women are battered each year. Most seek medical care, making battery the single largest cause of injury to women in the United States.*[1]

- *Twenty percent of visits by women to emergency services are due to battering.*[2]

- *Some form of violence occurs in 25 percent of all marriages.*[3]

- *Women are three times as likely to be victimized frequently as are men.*[4]

- *Wife abuse occurs in all socioeconomic groups, from very rich to very poor, highly intelligent to mentally retarded, from college-educated professionals to high school dropouts.*

One reason that the 1988 Joel Steinberg–Hedda Nussbaum murder trial for the death of their six-year-old daughter Lisa attracted so much attention was that the abuse occurred in a middle-class home. Hedda, a former children's book editor, was repeatedly punched and beaten by the man she lived with, lawyer Joel Steinberg. In the trial, the battered woman was granted immunity because she herself was thought to have been too severely beaten to have struck the blows that killed Lisa or to have intervened on the child's behalf.

But although it is true that abuse is present in all levels of society, there are certain so-called risk markers, or factors that carry an increased probability of abuse. These factors were highlighted in the largest survey dealing with wife assault—one conducted by telephone in the spring and summer of 1985 by Lou Harris and Associates.[5]

The survey found that income is the factor most consistently associated with wife abuse. Couples living at or below the poverty line have a wife-abuse rate substantially higher than that of most well-to-do couples. Among families in which the male partner was unemployed or employed only part-time, the level of severe abuse was two to three times as high as the level among families in which the male was fully employed.

The survey also found that husbands from minority groups had the highest rates of adult female abuse. The rate of wife abuse among black families was nearly 400 percent higher than the rate for white families—a relationship that can probably be explained by socioeconomic status. That is, minority and black husbands tend to have lower incomes, and it may be the effect of this factor, rather than minority status or ethnicity per se, that accounts for the differences in abuse rates. Finally, most husband-to-wife violence took place in families where one partner was under the age of thirty.

Extreme frustration sometimes leads battered wives to take the law into their own hands. And sometimes women who are threatened by a taller, stronger man resort to weapons as an equalizer. An estimated 74 percent of serious assaults by women come in response to attacks by their partners. Of women who killed their husbands, 60 percent did so in response to violence by their husbands. In contrast, only 9 percent of men killed their wives in response to violence inflicted on them.[6]

The same data also show that a gun in the hands of a woman is not as dangerous as the same weapon in the hands of a man. Where guns were fired in abuse situations, 85 percent of the men suffered only minor injuries, and only one man required hospitalization. By comparison, 46 percent of the women fired at needed to have their wounds medically treated.

Women are most often violent to protect themselves or their children. In New York State, according to the same report, women have sought about ten times as many orders of protection against their husbands as have husbands against wives.

SEXUAL ABUSE

Forced sex in marriage is a common form of sexual abuse, and one that has not been admitted to until recently. "The fact of the matter is one out of seven married women is raped by a spouse, but most are reluctant to come forth and talk about it," says the National Clearinghouse on Marital and Date Rape in Berkeley, California. "Women don't realize they have a right to say no to sex, even to a spouse."[7]

Most wives would resist calling it rape, thinking that rape is unwanted sexual experience between strangers. But according to the legal definition—"forced intercourse, or intercourse obtained by physical threat(s) . . . or when the woman was . . . totally helpless and hence unable to consent"—rape is a persistent problem in a large number of relationships.[8]

Women raped by husbands are traumatized at the most basic level. At the very least, the rape undermines the husband-wife relationship. But even more important, the violation of a woman's body can lead to serious psychological harm. An attack can destroy a woman's trust in others and leave her feeling even more powerless and isolated than if raped by a stranger. Eventually, the bad feelings may lead to psychosomatic illnesses and even to suicide attempts. The following case study illustrates one terrible outcome suffered by a victim of sexual violence.

Vera P. appeared at a local medical clinic on various occasions with complaints of difficulty in swallowing and also back pain. Doctors dismissed her complaints as psychosomatic and sent her home.

Although she never mentioned it, her husband continually assaulted her, physically and sexually. Over several years, she went to the emergency room again and again with facial fractures and symptoms of "blacking out" due to repeated head trauma. She also complained of depression and addiction to drugs. Eventually, she reached a point where she was taking twenty-five Valium pills a day to cope.

One day Vera decided to put an end to all the abuse by taking her own life. When the police came to her house, they found her suicide note: "I am frightened. No one can help me. My children and I live in danger. My husband repeatedly beats and rapes me. The police say they can't help me. I have been to the doctors many times. I sent my children to relatives, because I do not want them hurt. There is no other way to protect them. Please tell them I love them. I don't know any other way out."

Men use two basic justifications for marital rape. One stems from their belief that males have an overpowering need for sex and that this urge cannot be denied. The other comes from the feeling that women withhold sex for no good reason. Both attitudes arise from the idea that forced sex is mainly a response to a woman who refuses to satisfy the legitimate needs of her husband.

Although most people consider rape a serious offense, few regard the sexual assault of a spouse or former spouse as very serious. "A marriage license is a raping license" is one commonly stated view. For a wife, though, the trauma can be even worse since she usually continues to live with her husband. Often, the wife remains in the situation because she is unable to leave or to get help from the criminal justice system.

In one case, a housewife attempted to prosecute her husband for rape. She testified: "He put a shotgun to my head and told me that if I didn't have oral sex with him that the barrels of the gun were the last thing I would ever see. I believed him."[9]

Similar cases have attracted national attention and raised questions about a husband's right to rape his wife. Today, some states allow married women to bring charges against husbands who force them to have sex against their will. Twelve states offer no protection of this type.

In one study, 323 Boston-area women were interviewed. Ten percent said they had been forced to have sex with their husbands or partners. Violence accompanied rape in about one-half of the instances. Diana Russell, in *Rape in Marriage,* says that "14 percent of the 644 married women interviewed reported one or more experiences of marital rape. Other studies found that 3 to 10 percent of the married women surveyed had been raped by their husbands."[10]

THE ABUSERS

Although it is difficult to describe completely the man who abuses his spouse, the attorney general's report summarized some main characteristics.

Perhaps most important is the matter of size. Men who batter are on average forty-five pounds heavier and four to five inches taller than their victims. The men are more likely to have had experience in fighting, having been taught that it is manly to fight.

Men who abuse their partners generally show a lack of responsibility for their own actions. They probably believe all the myths about the battering relationship, such as the woman "caused" the incident. They blame the abused woman for the problem.

An abuser will make a woman feel guilty for behavior she has no control over. He will say, "If you loved me, you wouldn't mind if I drank, gambled, or had affairs." The emotional aspect of the abuse may actually paralyze many women from ever seeking an escape from the abuser. They feel, in some way, that they are to blame.

Assailants are generally unaware of the role stress

plays in their lives and often ignore signs that they are becoming stressed. When troubled, they use drinking and battering to cope. "He started really drinking excessively and that is when the abuse started." "He had been drinking. . . . I sat down to read the paper and he wanted his supper . . . he kicked the cat to the ceiling . . . he started slapping my face with both hands."

Offenders refuse to believe that their violent behavior will have negative consequences. They minimize and deny the seriousness of the violence. As a woman testified about her husband: "He's a very good liar. He looks very sincere. He promises anything you want to hear. He promises that he will do anything, lots of tears, and, 'I'm so sorry, and I love these children, I would never do it again.' You want to believe that it's just a mistake, but it's not a mistake."

In studies of motives, the leading issue is usually said to be jealousy. The husband, for example, may be pathologically suspicious, guarding against losing his wife, whom he mistakenly sees as a possession. Most assailants are unable to identify and/or express any emotion other than anger. They use aggression and violence to vent their angry feelings. Sex, too, is an act of aggression, frequently used to enhance feelings of self-esteem.

The man who batters is generally socially isolated, with few friends or close relatives. This may make him dependent on his partner for all emotional outlets and support. Any outside contact that his wife has with family or friends makes him envious.

Many men have difficulty dealing with independent women while trying to play the traditional male role they feel is expected of them. "Everybody tells you to control a household," said a man jailed for wife abuse. "But they don't tell you how. It isn't fair. They've changed the rules."

The assailant generally exhibits a pattern of controlling behavior. Usually, the man believes in male supremacy and plays the stereotyped masculine sex role of dominance in the family. This feeling of "ownership" lies behind most wife beating. The man strives to control the woman by various means and with varying degrees of success. At the same time the woman strives to resist the force. In some relationships, this brinkmanship may even lead to homicide.

Control is the cornerstone of an abusive relationship. Anger and intimidation are used, again and again, to manipulate the woman's behavior. An abuser will destroy valued personal items—heirlooms, clothes, pictures—to show what will happen if the partner tries to assert herself. He may kill or maim a pet to make a point. "He would do petty vindictive things, like accidentally breaking a vase that I particularly liked," recalls one formerly battered woman. "One day, he cut up all my lingerie into pieces."

A batterer often believes that he cannot show any "female traits." If he does, others will see him as less than manly. He truly thinks that violence is a masculine trait. The woman should always be the nurturer, the care giver, he thinks. When she is critical or demanding, he is justified in using violence to "keep her in line."

Insecurity in relationships is a common characteristic ascribed to abusers. The batterer often has a low opinion of himself. He sees others as worthless, therefore "abusable," because of his own feelings of worthlessless. More than half of all batterers also abuse their children.

Those who abuse women usually present a dual personality, alternating between extreme tenderness and extreme aggressiveness. They tend to avoid any situation in which their weak emotional skills will be discovered. And they are probably ignorant of the process of building a relationship. Unable to think through a situation, they are also impulsive. "There were times when he was very sorry and said it would never happen again, and it always did. I had black eyes, disconnected shoulders, bruises all over my body—I also had bald spots on my head from all the hair yanking," said one victim.

Women who decide to desert an abusive husband may be putting themselves at risk for their lives. This is what makes many abused wives reluctant to leave. Young wives are especially at risk. Their youth makes their husbands jealous; they believe that other men find their wives attractive. Also, young husbands may not be as deeply tied to their wives—and vice versa—as individuals who have shared many years of marriage. The looser connection may make for a less stable relationship and shorter marriage—and hence, greater violence.

Men are far more likely than women to commit suicide after killing a spouse; they are especially likely to do so when the couple is separated or divorced.

THE VICTIMS

Experts can find no common personality characteristics for abused women as they can for violence-prone men. They know that abused women are frightened. But most everyone believes that this fright is appropriate. A woman in a dangerous or life-threatening situation tries to avoid making the batterer angry.

"I could feel the bones in my face breaking," says one victim, "but I knew that if I were to move or to make a sound that I would die." She tries not to show her real feelings because she could get hurt for them. Her fears that separation will make the violence worse are usually accurate.

Hedda Nussbaum has come to epitomize the abused woman in our time. The testimony she gave offers some insights into her character and her nightmarish relationship with Joel Steinberg. For example, Hedda testified she "had worshiped Steinberg quite literally, believing that he possessed spiritual powers." She told the court that she believed that her happiness and survival depended on being the good wife. She "didn't want to show disloyalty to Joel."[11]

Experiences from childhood and those from living in a violent relationship may interfere with a woman's ability to stop the batterer after he starts the violence. As a result of living in a situation filled with violence, the woman may come to view herself with an altered self-image. She may come to believe the myths about the battering relationship, such as that she somehow was to blame for the assault.

Usually the beatings start gradually and escalate over the years the new couple live together. First, the woman considers the beatings accidents. Then she goes on to believe that they are something that she deserves or provoked.

To avoid being hurt, the woman may accept the traditional role at home and follow the batterer's expectations of proper behavior. She comes to accept her partner's opinion of her and assumes responsibility for her batterer's actions. Nussbaum testified that she did not live in physical fear of Steinberg. She accepted the beatings because "he said he was trying to help me, or he said I'd been lying to him, that I wasn't behaving in a manner acceptable to him."

No matter how horrible the beatings, no matter how much damage she sustained (broken jaw, broken nose, broken ribs, ruptured spleen, gangrenous leg, cauliflower ear), Hedda denied the abuse. She reportedly believed that violence "wasn't within [Joel's] character."

The abuser creates a situation in which the abused woman really thinks that she can't get along without the assailant. In one case, the husband of a struggling actress, who has since become divorced, insulted her constantly and discouraged all her attempts to get a job in movies or on the stage. He told her that she was too fat and too ugly to be an actress. When she didn't have any success with auditions, she decided he was right and after a while just gave up and stopped looking for work altogether. Eventually, she had no choice but to depend on him for financial support.

Limiting finances is another way abusive partners prevent a woman from gaining independence and thus escaping the violence. The victim is often forced to hand over any money she might earn. Property, such as an automobile or a home, is kept in the abuser's name, as are bank accounts. If the woman has no control over finances, there is no way she can start a new life.

WHY DO WOMEN STAY IN AN ABUSIVE RELATIONSHIP?

For many people, this is the biggest puzzle about domestic violence. It is a question to which there is no simple answer.

Although battering is a process that usually gets worse, there are still long periods of time when the partner is not violent. During these periods, the woman believes things will change. She thinks that she should try to help her husband and that together they will get through the hard times.

But abuse escalates and brings with it incredible psychological as well as physical changes in the victim. The woman is told, "If you leave you're dead." Or else, "Leave and you'll never see your kids again." By now she has every reason to believe he is serious. She feels trapped in a very violent relationship.

In one study, 114 women were asked why they stayed with the abuser. The three leading answers were as follows: [12]

Love (71 percent). Typically, once a woman realizes she's living with a truly violent man, much of her love turns to hate. What she continues to love, though, are the good moments, the times when he's not violent. She wants the relationship to go on, but without the violence, and he often promises her that she will have it again. "I love him," says one woman. "Besides, he's not always violent. At times he's charming, loving, and affectionate."

Fear (68 percent). Women might think of running away, but they may have nowhere to go or don't have enough money. Sometimes when they leave, their living conditions become worse. One woman moved into a rat-infested apartment that was so bad she returned to the batterer. Or, her husband stalks her and the kids, and she decides it is safer to go home. Leaving can be very dangerous. Women have been murdered by their husbands after deciding to leave the home rather than suffer further abuse.

Need (66 percent). Some women have been told for years that they cannot function without a man. They come to believe that statement. Such talk, heard often enough from the person with whom she is most intimate—her husband—makes the woman feel powerless and helpless. "It's important for me to have a man around the house and for my children to have a father," she says. "Whatever his faults, he pays the bills and looks out for us."

Many times the abused woman is like a lot of other people who believe that marriage is "for better or for worse." Her religious beliefs may prompt her to try her very best to save the marriage. Like so many women, the woman who is abused doesn't want the relationship to fail.

Relatives may urge her to remain with her mate. Also, a woman who has grown up with parental violence may have the impression that such behavior is normal and must be tolerated.

Many families find separation and divorce unacceptable. All of society's conventions and structures emphasize the value and importance of marriage, family, and motherhood. In so doing they act to keep the abused woman from leaving her husband and breaking up her home. Even public institutions and professionals in the community often fail to provide needed support and assistance. Not long ago, a husband tried to kill his wife. She called the police in desperation. Two policemen arrived and took a look at the house and at her bloodied face. They asked a few questions and then left shortly afterward, saying that her husband had the right to do whatever he wanted to do in his own home.

LEAVING A
BATTERING SITUATION

Women usually put an end to their abuse when they realize that the battering will never go away. It will only get worse over time. Since she cannot change the abuser's behavior, the wife decides she has to change the situation.

"What changes an abused woman's life," says one woman, "is when she starts to believe that she's worth something. I started hearing a voice inside of me again. It was the voice of my inner self. I hadn't heard it in a long time."[13]

Generally, there are three basic reasons why women leave a violent situation:

1. Knowledge that help is available.

2. Impact on the children. Living in a violent home where the batterer abuses the children physically, mentally, or sexually may give the woman the courage to leave.

3. Reaching the limit of violence she will tolerate.

"Everyone's bottom line is different," said Pat of Unity, a Maryland-based organization for battered women. Abused for twenty-five years of her married life, Pat finally left her husband when he spit in her face in front of company.[14]

Shelters are the main means of support for battered women who must leave their homes because of abusive husbands. Living in a shelter gives the woman an opportunity to obtain help from a variety of sources. "The greatest thing about being here is being safe," said a young woman whose husband threatened to kill her and their children. "I haven't slept so good for so long, knowing I'm not going to get hit when I wake up in the morning."[15]

In addition to providing a safe refuge, shelters help women gain confidence in themselves. They gain power in an emotionally supportive environment where they are able to make decisions for themselves.

By providing an opportunity for the woman to recognize herself as a valuable and worthwhile person, the shelter helps the woman raise her self-esteem. With help, she may even recover the feelings of self-respect, self-worth, and self-acceptance she had prior to the abusive situation.

Although the arrest of a violent family member is one of the most effective methods of dealing with spouse beating and other domestic crimes, it is no solution. Some offenders comply with orders to stay out of the home. Others go for counseling because they are afraid they will have to serve time in jail. Still others do not hesitate to violate these hard-to-enforce orders, especially if they have gotten away with it before.

Judges often sentence batterers to probation with a suspended jail term. Probation gives offenders a chance to avoid going to jail by meeting certain conditions. This may include attending a counseling program, complying with a protection order, and using no further violence. Men who attend workshops are taught techniques that help them to know when they are heading for a blowup, how to control it, and how to make basic changes in the way they live their lives. More often, though, the court order has "no teeth." It fails to monitor the offender, and so the process fails.

Offenders who violate conditions of probation sometimes serve a short period in jail. But even here arrest alone is not usually enough. After their release they often resume the abuse, sometimes more violently than before. In a pattern that is fairly typical, the offender will terrorize his wife, get arrested, post bond, and then return to attack her again.

In one recent case, twenty-nine-year-old Lisa Bianco had been beaten by her husband, Alan Matheney, over a period of ten years. The beatings continued even after Lisa obtained a divorce. After one particularly savage assault, Alan was imprisoned. Fearing his anger when he was released, Lisa pleaded with correction department officials to warn her if her ex-husband was to be set free. They failed to do this. One day, unknown to her, they issued her husband an eight-hour pass from state prison. Alan sneaked home and beat Lisa to death in front of the couple's two-year-old daughter.[16]

Even battered women who kill their spouses do not do well under the present criminal justice system. Most often—in 97 out of 100 cases cited recently—the women are sentenced to long terms in jail. Few are acquitted.[17]

Many believe that battered women are convicted because of a gender bias in the law of self-defense. The law is designed to deal with fights between two men of approximately equal strength. It does not know how to settle life-and-death struggles between two people of unequal strength who have a long-standing, intimate relationship.

Violence against women has always existed in male-dominated cultures. But attitudes are changing, and gradually wife abuse is being taken as seriously as assaults on strangers. As one woman testified at a public hearing: "Changes must be made in the attitude of the public towards the victims of domestic violence. . . . Every woman needs to be made aware that no one has the right to abuse her. No one."[18]

CHAPTER

5

CHILD ABUSE

■ *For years Terrence Karamba, nine, suffered dangerous thrashings by his father, a UN diplomat from Zimbabwe. On several occasions, the boy was hung from pipes in the basement and whipped.*

■ *Despite reports of child abuse from his grandmother, doctors, and day-care teachers, social workers decided to let three-year-old Matthew Eli Crackmore live at home. A few months later, the little boy was kicked to death by his father.*

■ *A mother charged with beating her child to death said in her own defense: "I didn't mean to kill the boy. I just wanted to discipline him."*

■ *A mother and her boyfriend were charged with second-degree murder after her five-year-old daughter was found dead with a possible skull fracture and bruises over her entire body.*

■ *A man was charged with killing his infant son by twice picking him up and throwing him to the floor. It happened after the man had been drinking heavily.*

■ *In the last weeks of her life, Tamake Green's father had repeatedly whipped her with an electrical cord, forced her to overeat until she threw up, and finally poisoned her.*

■ *Early one morning in November 1987, police found six-year-old Lisa Steinberg severely physically abused and barely breathing. The little girl was taken to the hospital, where she died a few days later.*

The National Committee for the Prevention of Child Abuse (NCPCA) defines physical child abuse as a nonaccidental injury or pattern of injuries to a child inflicted by a parent or other caretaker. These injuries include beatings, burns, human bites, strangulation, and immersion in scalding water. The injuries range from bruises and welts to broken bones, scars, serious internal damage, or even death.

When physical child abuse occurs, it is usually not an isolated incident. More often, it is part of a pattern of abuse that has been going on over a lengthy period. The effects usually grow worse with time. The longer the abuse continues, the more serious the results. Also, the more difficult it is to put an end to the mistreatment.

THE PROBLEM

At least 300,000—and perhaps as many as 600,000—children are victims of physical child abuse each year.[1]

Many physically abused children are even younger than six-year-old Lisa Steinberg. Forty percent of these victims are five years old or under. And nearly 75 percent of fatalities are in this age group.[2]

Nationwide, from 2,000 to 5,000 children die each year as a result of abuse.[3] Reports of child abuse nationwide increased 212 percent from 1976 to 1986 (perhaps due to better reporting), the last year that figures were available.[4] From 1985 to 1986 alone, there was a 23 percent increase in child-abuse deaths.[5] In some 30 to 50 percent of all childrens' deaths due to abuse, there was some prior warning that the child was at risk.[6]

In 1979 and 1980, the federal government conducted a National Study of the Incidence and Severity of Child Abuse and Neglect. According to this study, about 30 percent of all "maltreated" children are physically abused; others may be emotionally or physically neglected. About 10 percent of those who are physically abused suffer an injury severe enough to require medical treatment.[7] Four years later, the American Humane Association found a similar percentage of physically assaulted children in the survey that they conducted.[8]

Unfortunately, not everyone agrees on which acts can be considered abusive. On one side of the debate are those who feel that any act of violence, including a slap or a spanking, is harmful. On the other side are those who believe that strict discipline—up to and including corporal punishment such as beating—is necessary to prevent children from growing up "spoiled."

The First National Survey of Family Violence conducted by Richard Gelles and Murray Straus in 1976 showed an exceptionally high incidence of child abuse. Nearly two-thirds (63 percent) of the parents questioned mentioned at least one time when they abused their children during the year. Furthermore, three out of four parents said they struck their child one or more times during the course of the child's lifetime. More than half of the parents reported that they spank or slap their children each year; nearly half push, grab, or shove the youngsters in their care.

By combining all their data on violent abuse, the authors prepared what they call the Child Abuse Index. According to their findings, among children who range in age from three to seventeen, nearly forty of every thousand are victims of physical abuse. To put it another way, almost one boy or girl out of every twenty-two—or about one child in every single classroom throughout the entire

United States—has been spanked, slapped, pushed, grabbed, or suffered other rough treatment.[9]

In 1985, Gelles and Straus repeated their survey. Contrary to their expectations, the rate of abusive violence toward children had declined. Only nineteen children per thousand (compared to almost forty) were reported to be victims of abusive violence—a decline of about half. Yet, surprising as these new statistics are, they still show that millions of young people are victims of painful physical abuse.

THE VICTIMS

Children need a few basic essentials to be able to grow into mature, competent adults.

They need a feeling of power, to believe that they can have some effect on the world around them.

They need to know who they are and to identify with one or more groups so that they can feel secure.

They need to be accepted fully and without any conditions by their parents so that they can feel free to experiment, to test limits, and to make mistakes.

They need to be treated by those in authority with consistency so that they can come to believe that the world is a rational and predictable place in which to live.

They need to feel worthwhile and loved so that they can develop self-esteem and a good self-concept.

Children who are physically abused often suffer devastating consequences. They may become as socially deficient as the people who inflict the abuse. Abused children, especially boys, have a much greater chance of becoming involved in juvenile crime than children from nonabusive homes.

Here is one theory of how this happens: As a way of dealing with his or her poor self-image and feelings of insecurity, the abused child unconsciously begins to act like the violent parent. The parent is hostile, so the child becomes hostile. "The child says, in effect: 'If I make my-self in your image, you cannot hurt me as much' (fear of aggression), 'or walk away and leave me' (fear of loss of love). In many cases, the more violent and less loving the parent, the stronger the child's need to act like him or her."[10]

Abused children tend to show one of two personality patterns. They may be shy and uncommunicative. Or they may be nervous, aggressive, and destructive.

One common symptom of both personality types is a poor self-concept. Often, there is an inability to trust oth-ers, difficulties in getting along with both peers and adults, and general unhappiness. Many physically abused chil-dren see themselves as ugly, stupid, inept, clumsy, or in some way defective. In their art, abused children fre-quently draw themselves without arms and hands, a sign psychiatrists read as showing fear of their own anger and aggression.

When abusive parents turn on each other, the chil-dren often feel responsible for stopping the fights. Usu-ally they feel frustrated because they cannot do so. Not only are they terrified by the violence, but they are also frightened by their own sense of helplessness.

By the time they grow up, however, children who have been attacked by a parent or seen parents attack each other have learned a sad lesson. They themselves have learned to use violence to control people or situa-tions.

Many parents consider physical abuse the best way to discipline children. The outcome of such a pattern of behavior is often disastrous. To take one example: For much of his childhood, Brian received spankings from his father and appeared rather well behaved. But when he reached junior high school, he started hanging around with a wild crowd. His father escalated the punishment, using a belt and his fists to keep Brian "in line." But the more severe beatings failed to have the desired effect. One day Brian and his pals were caught breaking into a school and striking the janitor on the head with a bat. Brian was taken away from his father and placed in a foster home. Since then the boy has been in constant trouble with the law.

Until recently, some social workers and psychiatrists believed that removing the child from the home was enough to cure abused children. Youngsters were often placed in foster-care homes. Now experts say that abuse may have long-lasting effects and that removal from the home alone does not effect a cure. According to some experts, there are children who have been so severely abused from birth that they are unable to form emotional bonds in later life. Also, many children placed in other homes go on to suffer abuse at the hands of their foster parents.

The symptoms of child abuse are said to worsen as young people approach puberty—the age when their anger and pain often turn to violence and self-destruction. Adolescents may express their angry feelings by running away, stealing, lying, or setting fires. Sometimes they purposely set out to cause harm to other people, animals, property, or themselves—including suicide.

The link between abuse and homicide is especially clear. In one study of several youngsters who had committed murder, every one reported that he had been subjected to severe beatings as a child. Other evidence links *severe* punishment and later *serious* aggression. Two notorious examples: Charles Manson was the leader of a cult group that was responsible for seven murders in 1969. Later, Manson was found to have been severely abused as a child and rejected by institution after institution as an adolescent. Another young man charged with murdering five women was found not guilty because he was shown to be insane. His mental disorder was thought to have been created by the severe abuse he had sustained as a child.

Most studies of juvenile delinquents report high rates of abuse. The parents of delinquents generally show more cruel and inconsistent discipline, with far greater use of physical punishment, than parents of nondelinquents. A 1978 study involving 3,636 children reported as delinquent in New York State in 1971 and 1972 showed that almost 10 percent of the children had been abused compared to 2 percent in the general population.[11]

Experts have long suspected a link between abused children and a pattern of violent behavior when these children grow up. The most careful research on this subject was done by Edward Zigler of Yale University and his colleague Joan Kaufman. Although the results vary widely and are far from conclusive, they do show that about 30 percent of abused children grow up to become violent adults who abuse their offspring or their elderly parents. This is far greater than the average rate of abusive violence in the general population, which runs less than 3 percent.[12]

Nevertheless, individuals who have experienced violence as children need not necessarily consider themselves to be "walking time bombs." There is no reason to think that all victims of child abuse are liable to become suddenly violent. Such an attitude might lead to a self-fulfilling prophecy. Although the Yale University study did find that 30 percent of adults who were abused as children repeat the pattern of abuse, the remaining 70 percent did not.

THE DISABLED CHILD AND CHILD ABUSE

Disabled children constitute a particularly high risk group for abuse. But no one knows how many are abused because of their disabilities or how many are disabled as a result of abuse and neglect.

Physical abuse can result in neurological or orthopedic damage or in emotional or behavioral impairment. Of the 302 abused children in Dr. C. Henry Kempe's well-known 1962 study, 85 had actually suffered neurological damage, and 33 of the children had died as a result of their injuries. Another report showed that, out of 50 abused children, about 26 percent suffered permanent disabling conditions as a result of their beatings. Four were retarded, two had neurological damage, and seven had physical defects. Among 100 criminal offenders in Philadelphia, interviewers found a history of abuse in 82 of these young people; in addition, 43 remembered being knocked unconscious by one or the other parent.[13]

Not long ago a twenty-four-year-old man was charged in the beating death of his eight-year-old mentally retarded stepson. The man told investigators he had grown increasingly frustrated with the child's condition. The autopsy found that the boy had several fractured ribs, strangulation marks on his neck, and lacerations on his genitals.

Such frustration is not uncommon. Parents, teachers, and other adults sometimes expect youngsters with disabilities to perform at levels and behave in ways that are simply beyond their ability. Failure to meet unrealistic expectations may cause stress for everyone—adults and children alike—that not infrequently erupts into violence.

Experts recommend that parents of handicapped children be given special emotional and educational support. They should be fully informed about the child's limitations and about what they can reasonably expect. Furthermore, they should be encouraged to develop their child's potentials to the fullest—despite any and all restrictions.

Individuals sometimes decide to have a baby to save a floundering marriage or to force one partner to marry the other. In so doing, they may be putting their baby at risk for violence. Matters can become much worse for the baby who is born sick or disabled. A handicapped baby born to parents with a potential for abuse is almost certain to be the victim of violence or neglect or both.

THE ABUSERS

A number of different factors characterize parents or other caretakers who abuse children. No one list covers all the cases, but certain elements appear again and again.

Many parents who abuse their children come from homes where they themselves had poor parental models and were beaten or deprived as children. As parents, they lack the security that comes from having grown up in a good environment. They use violence as a kind of emotional release. As one batterer explained after inflicting a particularly severe beating on his young son: "I was so mad I could spit, but I felt better once I let him have it!"

Abusive parents rarely trust or turn to others when they need help. They are still fearful of being rejected or criticized, as they were when they were children.

Such parents often have a poor self-image. They see themselves as worthless, "bad" people. This may be the result of never having been able to please anyone. There is increasing evidence that social isolation and lack of family or friends are indicators of the potential for abuse.

Weak relations between husband and wife or boyfriend and girlfriend often typify people who would abuse children. The two people stay together more out of need and fear than out of love and happiness.

Frequently parents in abusive relationships believe in using violence as a tool for shaping behavior. "Babies should not be spoiled or allowed to get away with things." Or, "A good swat on the rear lets him know I mean business." Or, "What else am I going to do when he runs into the street or breaks something?" Such parents believe that children must be shown who is boss and made to respect authority or they will become stubborn and hard to manage.

Parents may view their child as "different" in some way. Sometimes the difference is real, as in the case of a disability, disfigurement, or retardation. But other times children are abused because of the parent's unrealistic demands. Perhaps the child annoys the parent because he is not mature enough to run errands or care for a younger sibling. Or it may simply be that the child has the "wrong" color eyes or an "aggravating" habit of thumb sucking or nail biting.

Certain patterns of parental behavior underlie much abuse and neglect. Heavy and frequent use of alcohol and other drugs or leaving children unsupervised are prevalent. They are also major causes of child deaths.

Maltreating parents tend to be among the very poorest people in the nation. Often this extreme poverty occurs in single-parent households where the mother either earns a minimum wage or is on public assistance. Experts claim that an estimated one-third of all abused children grow up in such circumstances.

Some suggest that the problem of child abuse has more to do with certain values in American culture than with individual differences. These values, they say, actually make it possible for child abuse to occur and are transmitted through such everyday cultural influences as television, the movies, and sports.

Other cultural patterns also impact on violence. First, there is the importance attached to self-reliance. Self-reliance often involves controlling other people, especially those who may lay claims on you. Without such control real self-reliance is not possible.

Another stresses a respect for authority and authority's right to use force if necessary to maintain itself. In American culture, a parent does not lose face for hitting a child. In fact, such parents may be deemed, and may consider themselves, better than others who do not physically discipline their children.

There is also the value placed on getting things done efficiently, with a minimum of effort. This results in a limit to the amount of time and energy adults will usually put into reasoning and persuasion—especially when they are trying to get children to do as they are told.

As we said, not all parents who were victims as children grow up to be abusers. What of these nonabusive parents? Which characteristics do they share?

Parents who break the chain of abuse usually have an extensive family and social support network in place. Furthermore, they are able to express their anger more openly than others. They feel freer about discussing their own abusive experiences. One conclusion that experts draw from the evidence is that the repetition of past abuse seems avoidable if help and support are made available.

THE LAW

Child abuse didn't receive widespread public recognition until 1962, when C. Henry Kempe coined the term *the battered child syndrome*. Between 1963 and 1968 the various states in the nation all passed child-protection legislation. The regulations required reporting and confirming of cases of child abuse and provided protective services for children.

By 1975 child abuse was known to be a problem affecting all of society. The Child Abuse Prevention and Treatment Act (1973) had been signed into law, and the National Center on Child Abuse and Neglect was in operation. The voluntary National Committee for the Prevention of Child Abuse had been established. In 1988 an amendment was tacked onto the Child Abuse Prevention and Treatment Act to provide additional aid for child-abuse prevention and treatment programs.

In the United States the legal responsibility for the identification and treatment of child abuse rests with the individual states. Thus, the laws vary from state to state. Each state has three kinds of laws that pertain to child abuse: reporting laws, juvenile court acts, and criminal laws.

Reporting laws indicate which incidents should be reported to state agencies and who is required or expected by law to report suspected incidents. Everyone must report incidents in which he or she has reasonable cause, based on observation or suspicion, of deliberate child abuse. Often, however, the line between what is accidental and what is deliberate abuse is difficult to draw.

Countless times every day neighbors, friends, relatives, and others witness incidents that might—or might not—be child abuse. "Shall we get involved?" they ask themselves. "Shall we tell someone what we have witnessed? Or, "Is it none of our business—and not really a case of child abuse at all?"

For example, here is a story that recently appeared in the *New York Times:* A neighbor heard screams coming from next door. A son and his father were having an argument. Suddenly the neighbor heard a banging. It sounded as if the father were bashing his son's head against the bathroom wall.

"I hope you kill me!" the boy shouted. "I hope you end up in jail for the rest of your life!"

The neighbor listened, not sure what to do. She considered calling the police. But soon it became quiet, and she decided to do nothing. Fortunately, in this case, the boy survived. But many youngsters are not as fortunate.[14]

As the fatal beatings of Lisa Steinberg and others have shown, many children are forced to suffer unspeakable horrors that sometimes end with their death. Advocacy groups now say that bystanders must overcome their reluctance to get involved. Not only must they report clear instances of abuse to the authorities, these groups insist; they must also take steps to prevent it.

Intervention by neighbors and relatives is often crucial in preventing further violence. Almost anything that can be done to ease the parents' sense of isolation and frustration may help—from offering to find financial or psychiatric assistance to easing the shame and anger that can lead to violence.

Most child advocates agree that anyone who has witnessed child abuse should inform the authorities. The parent need not have already seriously injured the child. It might be that a call will save the child's life.

Of course, many reports are unfounded or less than urgent. And there is not yet a systematic way of determining which child-abuse calls are truly necessary. But, as Patricia Schene, director of the American Association for the Protection of Children, says: "If you suspect [child abuse] and don't want to get involved, at least report. That's the minimum." [15]

All state laws require physicians and other professionals to report suspected child abuse. In most states, nurses, social workers, teachers, and day-care personnel are also required to file written reports.

The child-abuse reports are then forwarded to the appropriate state agency. If the child is thought to need protection or services, a social worker will refer the family to a service program. If the child needs emergency protection, the social worker can remove the child to a place of safety.

After the case is reported, the matter may come before a judge in juvenile court. The court may then order certain actions, such as removing the child from the home, ordering the family to participate in a treatment program, or bringing criminal charges against the offender.

The choice between returning the child to home under court supervision, placing the child in foster care, or terminating parental rights is an extremely difficult one. It is not a decision that judges make lightly. Before taking the child away, the state must show that leaving the child at home would expose him or her to serious risk. The standards for taking action in child-abuse cases also vary from state to state. New York State's law, which is typical, requires action only if there is a certain risk to the child's life or health.

But even when children are taken from their homes for protection, there are many problems. The foster-care system often has little better to offer children. And other lives often become severely shattered when a family is broken up.

On the other hand, delays can cause irreparable harm. In the Joshua DeShaney case, for example, a social worker judged the child better off at home than elsewhere, despite his father's brutality. As a result, the boy remained under his father's care. The abuse continued, causing Joshua permanent brain damage with profound mental retardation. Finally, the father was charged with abuse and sentenced to a little less than two years in jail. The boy is expected to spend the rest of his life in an institution.

The father was jailed because the abuse of children violates criminal law as well the juvenile code. The purpose of the criminal court is to determine if a crime has been committed and, if so, to impose the penalty sanctioned by law.

The laws have become more strict; but laws and courts cannot prevent child abuse. Everyone agrees that there is a limit to what the law can do. By the time a report is made or the law is implemented, it may be too late to do anyone much good. Instead of thinking of punishing people, many believe social agencies should concentrate on trying to prevent child abuse.

PREVENTION

Prevention seeks to remove the potential causes of child abuse. It is a slow process that requires a commitment from the entire community. It also requires a willingness to offer help to parents as well as to children.

Many prevention programs have been tried. Some have been found to be particularly promising.

One exciting approach offers support to new parents, such as perinatal bonding programs. The purpose is to lay a sound foundation for a loving relationship between mother and child. A strong attachment between the parent and the infant should be established at birth and continue to develop thereafter.

Parents Anonymous and other self-help groups teach people how to cope with the stresses of child rearing. Experts help parents find out what makes them angry and how to deal with that anger. Members of such groups usually say they fear losing control of their temper and the angry feelings they sometimes have toward their children.

Self-help groups reduce the social isolation that is so often associated with abuse. This is especially valuable for high-risk groups such as parents who have been abused, teenage parents, parents fighting poverty, or parents overwhelmed with responsibilities. Education can provide parents with information about child care and child development. Instructors can also inform new parents about social service and health agencies in the community.

Early and regular health care is an important way to identify and deal with physical and developmental problems in children, including those that might trigger abuse. It also serves to advise parents on well-child care.

Child-care opportunities, such as day-care centers and Head Start, make it possible for both parents to work. At the same time, these programs provide learning and socialization opportunities for children. Life-skills training for children equips them with the skills, knowledge, and understanding necessary to cope with crises of abuse, violence, and neglect.

Counseling and therapy programs for abused children minimize the long-term effects on children. They also reduce the likelihood of abused children later becoming abusive parents. Only when our nation sets a priority on these and similar programs can we hope to see an end to the terrible scourge that is child abuse.

CHAPTER

CHILD SEXUAL ABUSE

■ *A computer programmer, who was also a volunteer Big Brother, was arrested on sex-abuse charges involving his son and a neighbor's child. In the man's home police found files of pornographic pictures showing children engaged in various sexual acts.*

■ *A teenage girl reported her mother to authorities for forcing her to have sexual relations with the mother's boyfriend in exchange for a supply of crack.*

■ *A mother confessed to having a long-standing sexual relationship with her adolescent son.*

The legal definition of child sexual abuse varies from one state to the next. But according to the Surgeon General's Letter on Child Sexual Abuse, the problem occurs if a child—any person under the age of eighteen—is forced by physical or psychological means to engage in, or help someone else engage in, any sexually explicit conduct. This conduct includes actions that range from kissing and fondling to sexual intercourse.[1]

The terms *incest* and *rape* also have specific legal definitions. Incest usually refers to sexual intercourse between two closely related persons. Rape is the crime of having sexual intercourse with a woman or girl forcibly and against her will. Also, sexual intercourse with a girl under eighteen who is not married to the man is rape, even if she consents.

Young boys as well as young girls are common victims of sexual abuse. Girls are at higher risk in their own homes, usually from family members—a parent, brother, sister, or other relative. Boys are at higher risk outside the home and family unit—from a neighbor, family friend, babysitter, or teacher. As former Surgeon General C. Everett Koop warned, "The great majority of children are abused by someone they know and often trust."

THE PROBLEM

Although estimates of child sexual abuse vary considerably, one reliable source says that 22 percent of all Americans—that is, approximately 38 million men and women—have been child victims of sexual abuse! This shocking figure was based on a random national survey of adults questioned about their sexual experiences as children.[2]

If children today are subjected to the same incidence of sexual abuse as their parents and grandparents, says the same source, more than 13 million children (8 million girls and 5 million boys) will be sexually abused before they reach their eighteenth birthday.

Nearly one-third of the adults questioned had told no one of their experiences until adulthood; only 3 percent of the cases were ever reported to the police.

Twenty-eight percent of women who had been sexually abused had been abused before the age of fourteen; 12 percent were abused by someone in their families. Seventy-five to 85 percent of the cases of child sexual abuse involved a family friend or relative.[3]

The results of an important 1981 survey of Boston-area parents led by Dr. David Finkelhor, director of the Family Violence Research Program at the University of New Hampshire, was only slightly less alarming. In this study Dr. Finkelhor found, for example, that 15 percent of female parents and 6 percent of male parents reported sexual-abuse experiences in their childhood.[4]

Although the numbers vary somewhat from study to study, the conclusions are usually the same. Large numbers of children are victims of child sexual abuse. The number of reported cases is far below the number expected, based on estimates from the general population. And even these numbers are far below the true extent of the problem. Adults tend to repress, forget, or deny frightening or unpleasant sexual experiences they had in childhood.

Child sexual abuse takes many different forms. Yet Dr. Finkelhor found that there are several common characteristics present in most cases.

For example, the children do not consent to the abusive acts. They are made to believe that they have to obey the requests of adults. In many cases, the children have little or no understanding of what is being done to them. As one twelve-year-old girl said, "I never heard of any of the things he did."

The children often have mixed feelings about the abuse. In most cases, they would much prefer the sexual behavior to stop. Yet they fear the consequences of stopping. On another level, the victims want the rewards of extra attention and special privileges to continue.

The older person exploits the youngster. The adult uses his or her superior knowledge, skill, and strength to force the child into sexual behaviors. Children often believe offenders who tell them that such sexual activity is completely acceptable. The adult's unexpected behavior tends to throw them off guard. They don't realize that it is often within their power to say no to sexual advances.

Child sexual abusers almost always strive to keep their activities secret. Often, to be sure that there is no mention of their activities, they apply psychological pressure—threats, bribery, and intimidation. For example, in one day-care center where it was found that there had been child sexual abuse, the teachers brutally killed pet birds and gerbils in front of the children. They then told the children that the same thing would happen to them or people they care about if they revealed the sexual abuse. In other instances, the children's stuffed animals had been torn apart and buried. This was meant to be a warning as to how they would be treated if they told others what the abuser had done to them.

Those who practice child sexual abuse usually know exactly what they are doing. Intent is often the most important factor in deciding whether behavior is abusive. When the intent of the behavior is the sexual gratification of the adult, the situation is considered sexually abusive.

THE VICTIMS

All children—of every age, in every religious, racial, and socioeconomic group, and in communities of all sizes, urban and rural—are potential victims of sexual abuse. Nevertheless, some youngsters do seem to be at more risk for sexual victimization than others. Dr. Finkelhor prepared an inventory of the eight strongest factors in identifying situations where child sexual abuse is most likely. He calls it a Risk Factor Checklist:[5]

The presence of a stepfather. Women who had a stepfather in their childhood homes were six times more likely to have been abused than those living with a biological father. Some researchers have even begun to suspect that some stepfathers are "smart pedophiles," that is, that they marry women with families as a way of getting close to the children.

A period of time when the child lived apart from the mother. The danger of sexual victimization is three times greater if the child was separated from his or her mother for a length of time.

A mother who had failed to finish high school. When a child's mother has not reached a high educational level and is, as a result, less powerful in the family than the child's father, the child is at increased risk.

A mother who showed little physical affection to the child. Children who grow up in homes in which their mothers are emotionally distant and deny them love and the physical signs of affection are often at risk for sexual abuse. Some willingly go along with the abuse, trying to find a substitute for the love and caring they never had.

A family income of less than $10,000. A low income puts an added strain on the parents and may increase any problems or tendencies the mother or father has for sexual abuse.

Children with few or no friends. Small children whose working parents have left them in the care of teenage relatives or friends are another risk group. Lacking contacts with others of the same age, the children are often uncertain about normal and abnormal behavior. Sometimes they accept sexual abuse in the belief that it is normal behavior.

EFFECTS OF
CHILD SEXUAL ABUSE

Practically every study of sexual abuse stresses the harmful way it affects children. Some reactions may pass rather quickly, especially if the child is very young or if the victim is able to tell someone about the abuse. Other victims may suffer from persistent psychological problems, some of which may last a lifetime.

Experts have reported a number of childhood mental-health problems believed to be linked to sexual victimization. Many younger victims revert to infantile behavior, such as sucking their thumbs and wetting their beds. Some preteens experience depression, guilt, and learning difficulties and later may become sexually promiscuous and run away from home. Occasionally, victims set fire to their houses or mutilate their pets. A few even attempt suicide by shooting or stabbing themselves, by running in front of moving cars or inhaling exhaust fumes, or by jumping from the window or roof of a tall building.

Jon Conte of the University of Chicago compared 369 sexual-abuse victims with children who had not been abused. In general, the victims were more aggressive and fearful, less rational and confident, and more likely to withdraw from the normal activities of life. In addition, they had poor self-images and were much more eager to please adults. Other common symptoms included nightmares, headaches or stomachaches, memory problems, hysterical seizures, phobias, compulsive rituals, and various sorts of self-destructive behaviors.[6]

Studies have also looked at adults who had suffered sexual victimization as children. Here, too, there were certain common characteristics. In one survey more of the former victims were separated or divorced and had less satisfaction in adult sexual relationships than nonvictims. Victims growing up generally having a negative self-concept, often suffer from depression, have problems in interpersonal relationships, and exhibit inadequate social skills. Women who were abused as girls mistrust men, yet they enter into relationships with individuals who resemble the man who abused them as a child.

Some sexually abused children and some adults abused as children have major adjustment problems; others do not. Research has shown that the following factors tend to result in more serious aftereffects:

The victim is older at the time of the abuse.

The offender is older at the time of the abuse.

The offender is male.

Physical force is used on the child.

The incidents of sexual abuse occurred with some frequency.

The abuse occurred over a long period of time.

There was severe abuse, such as sexual intercourse.

The offender had a close relationship with the victim.

There were two or more offenders.

The victim's family was troubled by personal, social, or financial problems.

The victim had poor relationships with his or her brothers and sisters.

Psychological problems and physical symptoms resulting from the abuse may show up at almost any time, from right after the abuse to much later in the victim's life. They spring from the emotional trauma caused by sexual abuse itself and from the often intense pressure applied to the child not to reveal the abuse.

THE ABUSERS

The Finkelhor study discovered that child sexual abusers are related to their victims in the following ways: 43 percent are acquaintances, 30 percent are family members, and 7 percent are strangers. The sexually aggressive individuals are primarily male and either adolescents or adults.[7]

Nobody knows how many child abusers there are. Those who abuse children sexually are even less likely than their victims to talk about their experiences. Outwardly they look and act no differently than other men. As one expert says: "The child molester is neither a strong man nor a dirty old man in a wrinkled raincoat with a bag of candy. He typically knows his victims. He dresses and looks like everyone else."[8]

A 1985 Los Angeles study found that about one in every twenty-five men acknowledged sexually abusing a child. This figure, which is four times higher than the usual estimate of one offender in every hundred, means that there may be *millions* of child molesters in America.[9]

Although there are many theories of why child abusers develop a sexual attraction to children, nobody is sure of the exact reasons. Nicholas Groth, though, has classified child abusers into two groups: the "repressed" child abusers and the "fixated" abusers.[10]

The repressed abusers are adult males who have led an otherwise normal life until something happened to trigger the behavior. In one case, a man's wife returned to school to get a college degree, leaving him to run the household. Feeling lonely and abandoned, he turned to his daughter for affection.

The fixated abusers, on the other hand, have had a lifelong interest in children, making young boys or girls the main focus of their sexual thoughts and activities. This kind of abuser is usually unmarried and abuses other people's children. His actions are generally not impulsive but are carefully planned.

Experts have long searched for one common characteristic of most or all child abusers. In *By Silence Betrayed*, John Crewdson cites narcissism as such a trait. Although narcissists are commonly thought to be consumed with self-love, Crewdson describes how the extreme narcissist is really very insecure. Outwardly he may appear strong and successful. But inside he feels powerless and worthless. He tries to manipulate people and events so that he can get the affection and attention he so desperately needs. What the narcissist wants more than anything, Crewdson relates, is to be loved—even worshiped.

Such individuals prey on children because they can be controlled more easily than adults. Some say adults who have sex with children do so because they lack the skill to find sexual partners among their peers. One research project reports that 43 percent of child molesters are shy or show other social-skill deficits.[11]

Most abusers are able to convince themselves that what they do is neither harmful nor immoral. This is necessary to make the behavior possible. They may tell themselves, "A child who does not physically resist really wants and enjoys sex." Or, "Having sex with a child is a good way to show love and to teach the child about sex." Or, "Fondling a child's genitals is not really having sex, so no harm is done."

The abuser needs to believe that the child enjoys sex with him as much as he does with the child. Mike, thirty-eight years old, is an example. His "girlfriend" is only thirteen. Yet, like most other child abusers, he doesn't think he is doing anything wrong. He does not consider having sex with a "willing" girl an abnormal act.

The narcissistic theory helps to explain why abusers sometimes act on impulse and often perform degrading acts. They feel that the world revolves only around the satisfaction of their needs. The child victim of the moment can provide a "quick fix" to fill the abusers' inner void and emptiness. Such offenders have no feelings of affection or empathy for their victims.

Nearly all adults who have admitted to child sexual abuse were found to have been badly mistreated when they were children. In fact, many woman who were abused as children marry men who are abusers, and their husbands then go on to abuse the children of the marriage. One California study disclosed that as many as 90 percent of all mothers of victims were themselves victims of sexual abuse.[12]

THE LAW

Most legal actions against child sexual abusers begin when someone reports an incident. Usually the report is simply a telephone call to a child-protection agency or to the police. Such reporting is, of course, the responsibility of any citizen with information about or even suspicion of child sexual abuse. The authorities then try to determine the facts of the case and arrange for a physician to examine the child victim.

If the agency finds evidence of sexual abuse, it may take certain steps to protect that abused child. It may ask the court for permission to remove the child from the family and to appoint a guardian and an attorney to represent the child in court. Or it may ask the abusing parent to leave the home and have another family member look after the child. Removing children from their own home is a big step that courts hesitate to take. The evidence that the child was sexually abused must be overwhelming before most courts will make this decision.

If the police are convinced that a child has indeed been sexually abused, they take the information to the district attorney. Criminal charges are then filed against the alleged abuser. But there are many obstacles to the successful prosecution of child abusers. In most sexual-abuse cases, the only corroborating evidence that is likely to exist is medical. And such medical evidence is not always available and is often open to differing interpretations.

Thus, sexual-abuse cases end up depending on the testimony of the child involved. If the judge decides the child is capable of testifying truthfully, the trial proceeds. If not, the charges are dismissed. When the child is too young to testify, there is likely to be no case.

The defendant's lawyer can sometimes delay the trial for months, or even years. The longer the delay lasts, the less likely is the prosecution of the abuser. A dragged-out case is particularly arduous for the child. Also, childrens' memories often fade fast, and their testimony may become unreliable.

A skillful lawyer can easily confuse the child about

the time, place, and sequence of events. Given the word of a child versus the word of an adult, the jury is going to believe the adult, says one experienced lawyer.

Dr. Eli Newberger, a pediatrician and an authority on sexual abuse of children, feels that not enough concern is shown for the abused children in collecting evidence and having them testify. He recently declared that subjecting children to the trauma of pursuing child-abuse cases through the courts had itself become "an increasingly prevalent form of child abuse."[13]

As former Surgeon General Dr. C. Everett Koop has said, "The system tries to be fair" but it is often "bewildering and even intimidating."[14] Thus, 90 percent of all child-abuse cases are not prosecuted, with the unfortunate result that many suspects are released. Not only do they escape penalty, but they are then free to further abuse the victim or other children.

In one recent case, a man who had confessed to raping a child received a suspended sentence. At the trial it came out that the man was a teacher. School authorities knew that he had committed rapes in the past but had failed to report them. Only when he was accused of still another rape was he finally sentenced to prison.

Many workers in the field of child sexual abuse lack the time, training, and experience to do a good job. The agencies tend to be understaffed. And since child-protection workers are often overworked and underpaid, there is a high rate of turnover.

Some judicial reform, too, is needed to make it easier for child sexual-abuse victims to testify in court. The use in court of videotape instead of live testimony is currently authorized in fourteen states. It may be one important improvement.

Other reformers are asking that special hearsay exceptions be permitted in child sexual-abuse cases. This would allow certain out-of-court statements, which would not ordinarily be permitted, to be admitted as evidence.

So-called hearsay evidence would be useful when a child freezes in court or changes his or her testimony on the witness stand.

New steps also need to be taken to correct certain problems in family court. Consider this notorious incident: A mother, Dr. Elizabeth Morgan, found that her child, aged two and a half at the time, was being sodomized and raped by her father. Dr. Morgan brought the matter to family court. Eleven sexual-abuse experts confirmed the abuse. The judge awarded the mother custody of the child but ordered visitation rights for the father.

On the father's first visit the child reported being molested; after the third she told how she had been raped. Not quite five years old at the time, the little girl developed suicidal tendencies. Fearing for the child's health and safety, the mother violated the visitation order and hid the child from the father. For this action, Dr. Morgan was sent to jail. She had been in jail for more than one year—all for trying to protect her child from further sexual abuse.[15]

PREVENTION

Dr. Finkelhor's 1981 detailed study of 521 parents showed that they have a hard time talking about sexual assault with their children. "If I ask my son to a sit-down talk, he will know immediately that we're going to talk about something I'm uptight about," says one father. Parental feelings play a big part in how they handle the subject. Some would rather talk about death, suicide, or abortion—any subject other than that of sexual abuse. When asked why they avoid the topic, they say it is because there is little chance their child will be abused, he or she is too young, or the subject is simply too frightening.[16]

As Dr. Finkelhor's research points out, sexual abuse can start very early—when children are as young as two months old—even though the most common onset is between six and eight years of age. Yet most parents of very young children in the study chose nine as the best age to talk about sexual abuse. Those who had nine-year-olds picked age ten. And so on.

Almost all parents warn their children to watch out for strangers: "Don't take candy from a stranger," "Don't accept a ride from someone you don't know," "Don't let a stranger into the house," and so on. Yet very few realize that these are extremely rare events. Children are at far greater risk of sexual abuse by people known to them. Warning only about strangers, some say, leaves children even more vulnerable to child abuse.

Without a doubt, the primary way to prevent child sexual abuse is through education. Children need to be taught how to prevent or escape their own sexual victimization. Important concepts that must be impressed on youngsters include the following:

Your body belongs to you. You can decide who touches it. Children have a right to control access to their own bodies. They do not have to allow anyone to handle, examine, or use their bodies in any way.

Not all kinds of touching need to be accepted. There are "okay" and "not okay" touches. The basic idea is that if it feels funny, embarrasses you, or makes you uncomfortable, it's not okay. In those cases, you're justified in refusing permission.

It's a good idea to tell someone. It's important for children to know that they can come to adults to report any suspicion of sexual assault. Recently, an eleven-year-old girl burst into tears and ran from the room after viewing a school film on sexual abuse. She later confided to her teacher that her two brothers had been abusing her sexually for four years, but she had been afraid to tell anyone about it.

Trust your own feelings. Children should learn that if they get the feeling that something is wrong or inappropriate about a situation, they are probably right and should tell someone.

Sometimes secrets are hiding things that shouldn't be hidden. Parents and teachers should point out that not all secrets are the same. Secrets among friends or classmates are fine. But secrets children are asked to keep about sexual activities are not. There are also differences between gifts given without conditions and gifts that have a price, which are really bribes.

It's not your fault. Children have to know that they are not to blame for not stopping someone from touching them in a sexual way. Sometimes it is impossible for youngsters to force adults to leave them alone. Through playacting, though, children can be helped to deal with the embarrassment or feelings of guilt that may follow.

Experts suggest that parents and grandparents, other close relatives, teachers, and parents of friends are the likely adults to be told of sexual abuse. The adult should accept the child's word unless there is conclusive evidence to the contrary.

Child sexual abuse is a complex problem with no one cause and no one "cure." There is still no complete and accurate profile of the child sexual abuser. And no one method has been found to ensure against the many forms of child sexual abuse. Thus, researchers continue to study ways to prevent or forestall such actions.

Despite the startling rise in the number of child-abuse reports, from 150,000 in 1963 to more than 1.3 million in 1982, there is evidence that reporting laws are not working as well as they might. According to a federal-government study, fully two-thirds of all cases of suspected child abuse are not being reported. This includes 87 percent of those cases known to teachers and other school personnel.[17]

A 1988 New York City study found that 25 percent of the city's teachers, 18 percent of hospital workers, and 8 percent of police officers had failed to report at least one case of suspected child sexual abuse. The teachers were asked why they failed to contact the proper authorities.

Their responses expressed the fear of making parents angry, involving themselves in the criminal justice process, or being proved wrong.[18]

When teachers intervene, however, future abuse can be prevented. Recently a six-year-old boy told his mother that his older stepbrother was abusing him sexually. She ordered the young boy to stop telling lies. So the boy decided to tell his teacher. Only then did the mother take her son seriously and force the stepbrother to move out.

Doctors, too, are often reluctant to file reports. As one doctor put it, "Unless you do it anonymously, reporting puts you in the position of being further involved in what happens. Quite often the lawyers and sometimes the courts are not very considerate of your time and of what this costs you."[19]

Most of those who abuse children do so, in part, because they believe they will never be found out. Better reporting of sexual abuse might increase the abuser's fear of being caught. Making individuals liable for failing to report incidences of child sexual abuse is another way the legal system can help to protect children.

Organizations that care for children should obtain extensive background information on prospective employees. They should check all their job applicants for any child-abuse arrests or convictions. And finally, all organizations dealing with children should train and supervise their staffs to recognize and report any signs of child abuse.

Simply stated, child sexual abuse exists because molesters do not know how to stop themselves. It is frequently very easy to accost children in unprotected situations. And often the victims do not know how to resist abuse. Prevention needs to address all of these issues.

TREATMENT

The usual follow-up to a report of sexual abuse is a thorough medical exam. The doctor must be sensitive and well trained, with a good knowledge of what to test for. Usually this depends on the age of the child and the type of assault. The evidence that is collected is used in any future prosecution of the offender.

Police and prosecuting attorneys have the responsibility to protect the victim and society from the offender. In incest cases, separation of the victim and offender is virtually the only way to keep the victim from being pressured to change his or her story.

For the person arrested for abuse, pretrial diversion programs are becoming very popular. Incest offenders who admit their guilt can choose to undergo psychotherapy rather than be sentenced to serve time in prison.

Quite often a holistic treatment approach is used. Such treatment is based on the premise that sexual abuse is symptomatic of other problems. Treatment may be designed to help the abuser learn to handle stress and to empathize with others, work out his troubled relations with his wife or his employer, or break an addiction to alcohol or drugs.

Help is increasingly available now. The fact is that nationwide treatment programs have increased by more than 66 percent since 1986.[20] Sometimes, the solution is marital counseling or Alcoholics Anonymous (AA) to repair the troubled dynamics within the family. The whole family undergoes counseling together in an effort to raise the self-esteem of the father, mother, and victim. The family is reunited when everyone is convinced that the abuse will not occur again.

CHAPTER

7

ADOLESCENT SEXUAL ABUSE

■ *A fifteen-year-old girl testified that her father had raped and sexually molested her repeatedly over a two-year period. He told her that "a father should do this to a daughter."*

■ *A husband and wife and their fourteen-year-old son were charged in a series of sexual incidents involving the couple's eleven-year-old daughter.*

■ *A forty-five-year-old father of five was convicted of molesting his teenage daughters for fully half of their lives. As a result, two of the older daughters are in foster care. One thirteen-year-old daughter is being kept in the county children's shelter.*

■ *Two fourteen-year-old runaway girls were beaten and raped after they were picked up while hitchhiking. The girls refused treatment, however, fearing that if their physically abusive parents were notified they would face more beatings at home.*

■ *A thirteen-year-old girl went to the local police station to ask for protection from her father, who had forced her into an incestuous relationship with him for the past five years. Although the girl had told others about what had been happening, her mother refused to believe her, and her relatives refused to help.*

Experts have long recognized the connection between sexual abuse and other problems among adolescents, such as drug taking, alcohol abuse, suicide, running away, and prostitution. A better understanding of the whys and wherefores of adolescent sexual assault is one way to help put an end to this widespread form of family violence.

THE PROBLEM

Adolescents, ages twelve to eighteen, are particularly vulnerable to all kinds of sexual victimization, including incest and rape. At the same time, adolescents themselves are perpetrators of sexual assault in growing numbers. Both problems receive very little attention in this country. Yet each year tens of thousands of young Americans are affected.

Adolescence is, for many, an especially stressful time. Within a period of only a few years, the young person is transformed from a child into an adult. There are changes in body function, physical appearance, moods, and feelings. Strong sexual feelings, the growth of peer attachments, a striving for independence, and a search for personal identity become quite strong. Opposite-sex friendships, dating, romantic attachments, and sexual experimentation grow increasingly important. With so much going on, it is not surprising that any form of sexual victimization can easily disturb adolescent development and produce serious and lasting effects.

Although victims of sexual assault range from infants to the elderly, the average age is slightly under twenty. Fifteen years is the age that is most frequently reported.[1]

INCEST

Incest is now known to occur much more frequently than previously imagined. For example, some figures show an annual incidence of about 300 cases per million. Compare this rate to 1968, when there were fewer than two cases per million. Among the most commonly reported instances of incest are between a girl and her father, stepfather, or mother's boyfriend. Incidents between mother and son seem to be least likely to occur.[2]

Incestuous relationships usually involve the oldest daughter and start when she is about ten years old. The relationship may continue for years and, in some cases, may be inherited by a younger daughter when her older sister leaves home. In most cases the father gains the daughter's participation through devious means, which may involve the use of his authority, pressure, and persuasion or the misrepresentation of moral standards. Usually the daughter offers no physical resistance to her father's increasingly aggressive sexual advances.

Among adolescent incest victims, psychological or social withdrawal is the most characteristic reaction. This is especially true when the victim has been pledged to secrecy and has kept this promise over a long period of time during which there were repeated sexual encounters. The incest secret becomes a symbol to the girl of something important that separates her from other people. Fear of exposing the secret interferes with her interpersonal relations. And social isolation interferes with her development. Without sharing secrets, fantasies, and significant experiences with friends, the adolescent has more difficulty in achieving a personal identity.

Studies show that incest may result in serious confusion over sexual identity and may lead adolescents to fear their own sexuality. Many react with hostility, anxiety, guilt, and depression. Such girls may have learning difficulties or physical complaints, attempt suicide, or become sexually promiscuous. Others may develop other behavior problems, including delinquency and drug or alcohol abuse.

Young people who have been pressured into continuing sexual activity with an adult often get used to providing sexual services in exchange for a variety of rewards. This learned behavior becomes part of a pattern that may eventually lead to prostitution for both boys and girls.

Incest victim Barbara Myers wrote this account of her experiences: "I felt marked. I knew that, wherever I went, men would find me and abuse me. So, my attitude toward prostitution was, 'Why not?' If I had to have sex, I thought, why not get something for it? I felt that I deserved the money: other men were going to have to pay for every time my father had me."[3]

Quite often, adolescents will try to remove themselves from incestuous situations by running away. In fact, more than a million children run away from home in the United States every year, according to a report issued by the Department of Health and Human Services. Most of these children are victims of sexual or physical abuse. A 1987 survey found that 61 percent of runaway youngsters had been abused, 51 percent of them by a parent.[4]

As Ms. Myers explained: "I never thought about where I was running to—only what I was running from. I didn't care where I was going or with whom. I was looking for anyone to take care of me and protect me from my father."

The big problem for adolescents living on the streets is by now well known: Once on the streets, these victims of abuse become vulnerable to further violence and sexual exploitation either through pornography or prostitution.

Delay in reporting incidents of adolescent sexual abuse is more common than not. This fact was confirmed in another study of over forty-four victims, which found that there were at least two or more incidents of sexual assault by a family member before the matter was brought to the attention of the authorities.[5]

When a father is accused of incest, the mother often

reacts with feelings of guilt and shame. Not infrequently she completely denies any knowledge of the matter. Another reaction is to accuse her daughter of lying or of purposely tempting and provoking the father.

The father's remorse and fear of repercussion may be equally overwhelming. This leads him to vigorously deny his daughter's allegations. He may join the mother in threatening to reject the daughter and make her feel guilty for destroying the family. Given this state of affairs, many young victims feel they have no choice but to retract their stories.

Those that report have a chance of receiving treatment. In the treatment of incest, therapists focus on the family and consider the incestuous relationship as a symptom of deep-seated problems in the home. The goal is to lessen the impact of the crisis and to reinstill a feeling of family unity. The worker first tries to put an end to the incest and then works on decreasing the guilt and anxiety experienced by the family members who are involved.

Identification and treatment of incest can serve as a measure of prevention since there is some evidence that incest may be passed from generation to generation. Case histories show that mothers and fathers who have incestuous relationships with their children often were themselves victims of incest as children.[6]

Also, the recurrence of incest after disclosure is highly unlikely. The main exception, curiously enough, is in those cases where the father or the child is temporarily removed from the home. The incestuous relationship usually resumes when the family is together again. Thus, imprisonment of the father or placement of the child in a foster home or shelter is not considered adequate treatment in and of itself.

In cases where long-term supportive services are made available to both the victims and the offenders, such help has made a significant difference in the lives of all of the family members. It has made it possible for the family to come together again and function as a healthy social unit.

RAPE

That rape victims are disproportionately teenagers is sometimes blamed on the turbulence of adolescence. The sexual maturation, the loosening of family controls, the reaching out for new identities, ideals, experiences, and friends among peers all seem to make teenaged girls particularly vulnerable to sexual assault.

Generally speaking, rape is viewed as a complex act that is mainly an expression of either anger or power. In so-called anger rape, the offender uses the sexual act to release the pent-up anger and rage he feels against others. The assault is usually accompanied by physical brutality. Sex is the weapon the offender uses to degrade his victim. He seeks to hurt and sees punishment and humiliation as ways of getting back at those important persons in his life whom he believes have wronged him.

In power rape, the main factor is to exercise control over another person. Most incest cases fall into this category. Sexuality becomes a way of making up for underlying feelings of inadequacy. It serves to express the rapist's fantasies of mastery, strength, and authority. The offender has a desperate need to reassure himself about his adequacy as a man. Rape allows him to feel that he is in control of someone else. Through rape he hopes to deny his own deep-seated feelings of worthlessness and vulnerability and to shut out disturbing doubts about his masculinity.

Rape, or any other kind of sexual assault, is always a frightening, ego-shattering experience that leaves the victim feeling extremely helpless. To make matters worse, rape has been mistakenly viewed as something that lessens the worth of the victim and is the victim's fault. This traditional attitude has made some mistakenly think it socially unacceptable to tell others about the experience. A study that collected data from 468 young rape victims over a period of three years found that the adolescents were reluctant to tell their parents of the incident. They mainly feared that they would not be believed or that the family members would blame them.[7]

In rape situations, adolescent victims often encounter negative reactions that cause further stress for the victim. The term *second wound* refers to the trauma unwittingly imposed by people who deal with the victim after the initial crisis.[8]

How well the adolescent recovers from the assault usually depends on his or her background and level of maturity as well as support from family and others. Adolescents who hide their feelings and experiences from others usually have an especially difficult task of recovering. Sharing is extremely important.

ACQUAINTANCE RAPE

A recent National Crime Survey (NCS) reported that for girls between the ages of twelve and fifteen, sexual victimization occurred at the rate of 2.5 cases per 1,000. But this rate jumped sharply to 5.7 cases per 1,000 for females between the ages of fifteen and nineteen.[9]

Like younger children, adolescents are particularly vulnerable to sexual assault by a person known to them. This crime is often referred to as acquaintance rape. The offender may be a relative or someone who dates the victim, lives nearby, or has contact with the adolescent through school, sports, clubs, jobs, and so on. Quite often the offender is another adolescent of the same age or slightly older.

Dating members of the opposite sex is one way that young persons test their emerging sexuality and social skills. How smoothly these relationships go depends on the attitudes the young people bring to the situation. Unfortunately, violence and sex are closely intertwined in our society. Some American youngsters, therefore, grow up regarding forcible sex or rape as part of normal heterosexual relationships. For those with this attitude, a date becomes an occasion for sexual victimization.

Males and females receive different socializing influences while they are growing up. Females are taught that femininity means being soft, nonassertive, and dependent on men. The woman's goal is to be alluring and attractive, yet sexually unavailable. Also, women are expected to set the pace in sexual situations. Males, on the other hand, are brought up to think of themselves as strong, powerful, and aggressive. Many grow up believing it is their role to try to overcome a woman's resistance to sexual overtures.

A recent study of 432 Los Angeles–area adolescents illustrates the traditional view many still hold of sex roles. Boys equate sex with having power over girls. And girls, when they agree to sex, are "giving in," or relinquishing control. Most girls in this study tended to view the sexual relationship as one of romantic involvement, which includes warmth, tenderness, and caring. Meanwhile, most boys viewed a sexual encounter as a short-lived experience—one that has little to do with the future of the relationship or romantic feelings.

On the issue of the use of force to achieve sexual intercourse, the findings were also quite revealing. Both males and females said they believed that force is "all right" under certain conditions, especially when a girl leads a boy on or gets him sexually excited.[10]

Between 22 and 67 percent of dating relationships involve some kind of violence among high school and college students. More than one-quarter of the victims and nearly one-third of the offenders interpret violence in dating relationships as a sign of love. Many believe that love and violence should go together in intimate relationships.[11]

Typically, sexual attacks happen quite unexpectedly on a social occasion, such as a date or party. The offender escalates the warm and friendly relations into an attack. Often it occurs at a time in a girl's life when she is reaching out for friends. Instead of friendship, however, she finds herself in a situation that is out of her control.

Permissive attitudes about forced intercourse, plus the reluctance of courts to treat juvenile sex offenses as serious crimes, may be partly responsible for the aggressive tendencies of some young males. Most studies of adolescent sex offenders show that the offenders are usually in their mid-teens, white, of average intelligence, acting alone, and targeting slightly younger victims. An overwhelming number know the victim at least casually. More than half had been involved in a previous offense—but one that had not been punished by referral or commitment.

Not only are teenagers at risk for rape by a friend or acquaintance, but there is also a danger of victimization by more than one attacker. Gangs are often part of a neighborhood's teenage culture. And adolescents are sometimes the prey of a number of gang members. Very commonly, adolescent rape victims are attacked by two or more young males, with the offenders from the same community as the victim.

A survey of sexual assault among adolescents by Suzanne Ageton revealed that only 22 percent of the victims chose to tell their parents about incidents of acquaintance rape. The reasons they gave ranged from wanting to protect the family from upsetting news to believing that the family would not understand and blame the victim for the rape.[12]

After the brutal subjugation of acquaintance rape, the adolescent victim may turn away from all friends. Once the immediate danger of the attack has passed, she may consider herself dirty and contaminated, begin to worry about venereal disease and pregnancy, and lose much of her confidence and spontaneity. In addition, fearful and negative feelings grow immeasurably, and there are usually substantial changes in eating and sleeping habits. Without help, these responses and effects may last a very long while.

STRANGER RAPE

Not long ago, FBI national crime-reporting statistics showed that an estimated 34.4 out of every 100,000 females in the country were reported rape victims at the hands of strangers, a 94.2 percent increase over 1971. Since adolescents are often reluctant to report rape, the actual rate is thought to be considerably higher.[13]

In one type of stranger rape, several male teenagers attack a single victim. Recently, a fifteen-year-old girl was playing with a group of neighborhood friends. Suddenly, four youths, also from the neighborhood, started chasing the girls, who all fled. The boys chased the girls for a couple of blocks before they caught one girl. The gang of males twisted the girl's arm and forced her into an empty building. They then raped her and threatened her if she told.[14]

In this case, though, the victim told a girlfriend, who in turn told her mother, who then told the victim's mother. The victim's mother reported the rape to the police and brought the girl to the hospital for an examination. The police investigated but did not press charges. The detective said: "I tried to explain to the mother that it would be a difficult case in court. The boys would deny that they forced her. It would be a strain on the daughter to have to describe what happened."

Although the boys were not prosecuted, the adolescent who reported the rape was then helped to deal with feelings and reactions to the incident. A therapist showed her how to recognize the symptoms of distress—increasing signs of anxiety, long periods of silence, and physical pain. He helped her work through behavioral changes, such as irritability, avoidance of friends, and changes in her attitudes toward school. Eventually, she overcame her fear of being alone and going outside. And finally, she rebuilt her feelings of self-confidence and self-esteem, bringing to an end the paranoid feelings and nightmares of violence that had been tormenting her.

Figures drawn from many sources show that few rapists accused of committing an attack are ever convicted of the crime. On average, only slightly more than half the stranger-rape cases that are reported result in the offender's arrest. Most of the rapists convicted of attacking victims over twelve years old are found to be either teenagers or young adults up to the age of thirty.[15]

ADOLESCENT SEXUAL OFFENDERS

Although many adolescents are the victims of sexual assault, a certain number actually perpetrate such crimes. The exact number of sexual offenses committed by adolescents is not certain. But there is growing evidence of the problem's dimensions. Because these statistics deal only with reported cases, the actual figures may be much higher.

About half of the sexual-abuse perpetrators now coming into treatment are adolescents. Most adult offenders admit to beginning their patterns of abusive behavior during adolescence. One-half of male sexual-abuse victims now in treatment and one-fifth of females were abused by adolescents.

Historically, adolescent sexual offenses have not been taken very seriously. A Colorado judge once dismissed the charges in a gang-rape case with the explanation "Boys will be boys." Or, in some instances, the defendants have been urged to plead guilty to an alternate charge, such as assault, rather than be labeled a "sex offender."

The 1970s saw the advent of more effective treatment programs for adolescent sexual offenders. Treatment approaches that proved successful with adults are now being adapted to the special needs of troubled adolescents. Presently, though, there are only a few programs nationwide for preventing sexual abuse among adolescents.

The arrest rate of adolescents for rape has more than doubled since 1976, as has the number of arrests for other kinds of sexual assault.[16] Long-term incarceration, with psychotherapy directed toward impulse control and the learning of appropriate social and sexual behaviors, has been successful with a small proportion of adolescent sexual offenders. There is generally a better chance of success if the offenders accept the need for treatment and if they have the backing and support of their families. Community supervision following a course of institutional treatment and the deterrent effect of possible reincarceration have both been cited as important factors in successful rehabilitation.

One of the most important elements in preventing adolescent sexual abuse involves learning certain facts that everyone needs to know:

■ *Any sexual activity forced on a person against his or her will is a crime, whether it is called incest, rape, sexual abuse, or some other name.*

■ *No sexual abuse is the fault of the victim, no matter whether the assault was by a stranger or someone known and even if it happened when doing something with obvious risks, such as hitchhiking.*

■ *It is very important to get medical care as soon as possible after a sexual assault. Conditions may develop later that cannot be felt or known right after the attack.*

■ *Adolescent survivors of violent sexual crimes can—and should—contact a local rape crisis center or the National Organization for Victim Assistance, 1757 Park Road, N.W., Washington, DC 20010. (202) 232-8560.*

CHAPTER

ELDER ABUSE

- *A sixteen-year-old boy, addicted to crack, stabbed his mother to death after she refused to give him any more money to pay a drug dealer. The young man admitted he had killed her after they had an argument that got out of hand.*

- *Joseph Bertolotti, fifty-four, was arrested on charges of beating his elderly mother, seventy-five, and stepfather, eighty-six. Bertolotti had hit and threatened to kill his parents for refusing to sign over to him the rights to their home as well as their life savings.*

- *A New Jersey woman and her nephew were charged in the killing of her father. The motive apparently was greed. The daughter promised to share a sizable inheritance with the nephew.*

- *A grandmother was forced to raise two children after they were abandoned by her son and daughter-in-law. Yet her son violently attacked her when she accidentally received a check intended for him.*

Although most older Americans receive the support and respect of their children, others are not so fortunate. Typically, elder-abuse victims are parents and grandparents who are victimized by their spouses, children, or grandchildren. In most cases they are too terrorized or ashamed to speak out. Some may be too frail to defend themselves.

Elder abuse is a phenomenon about which very little is known. Only a small percentage of those who are abused report their victimization. The elderly must often rely on others to report incidents of mistreatment. Many protections now available to wives and children are unavailable to older victims. And not all states have laws requiring mandatory reporting to protect victims' rights. Families and the community seem ignorant of the problem and indifferent to the needs of older Americans.

THE PROBLEM

The problem of elder abuse is becoming more and more serious as Americans are living longer than ever before. According to the most recent report on elder abuse by the U.S. House Select Committee on Aging, about 3 percent, or "over 1,000,000 older Americans are physically, financially and emotionally abused by their relatives or loved ones annually."[1]

The actual prevalence of mistreatment may be much higher, some experts say, because most studies only involve elders living within a community and not those in institutions. There is also a tendency to underreport when dealing with a sensitive subject. Furthermore, the studies rarely deal with instances of "self-abuse," cases where people are just too weak or confused to meet their own needs.

Sociologists Karl Pillemer and David Finkelhor of the University of New Hampshire's Family Research Laboratory surveyed abuse and neglect among 2,020 elderly persons living on their own or with their families. The study found that less than 0.5 percent of the elders were neglected, while 1.1 percent were the victims of verbal abuse and 2 percent of physical violence.

Pillemer and Finkelhor define abuse as at least one act of physical violence of a person over the age of sixty-five—from a slap, punch, scratch, or bruise to a bloody nose or broken rib. Abuse also includes "chronic verbal aggression," where the elder was insulted or threatened at least ten times in the preceding year.[2] Neglect is the deprivation of assistance needed for important daily activities. For example, in the survey they describe a daughter's refusal to help her disabled eighty-five-year-old father and terminally ill, arthritic mother with household chores and shopping. She would sometimes leave them without food for days on end.

The three main categories of elder abuse are psychological, financial, and physical.

Psychological abuse has to do with inflicting mental anguish on the victim. Examples are name-calling, treating the person as a child, insulting, ignoring, frightening, humiliating, intimidating, threatening, and isolating the older person.

Financial or material abuse involves the illegal, or unethical, exploitation and/or use of funds, property, or other assets that rightfully belong to the older person.

Physical abuse is causing pain or injury to the older person or confining someone against his or her will. The common examples include hitting, pushing, shoving, physically restraining, or sexually molesting.

Any form of mistreatment of the elderly can result in severe harm or even life-threatening situations. Therefore, all forms of abuse pose extremely serious problems.

Some cases of elder mistreatment are not intentional, but many others are. These may be serious enough to be considered criminal behavior. The abuse usually results from such factors as greed, a mental or physical disability of the care giver or dependent, exhaustion of a family's financial resources, a history of family violence or criminal behavior, or alcohol abuse by the caregiver or the dependent. Where there is a combination of causes, the chance for mistreatment increases.

THE ABUSERS

The Pillemer and Finkelhor survey found that much elderly abuse is by the victim's husband or wife. Among the maltreated elders, 65 percent were abused by their spouses, while only 23 percent were abused by their children.[3]

"A lot has been made of children being saddled with elderly parents and the conflict that can arise from that situation," Dr. Finkelhor notes. "What we see here is the more serious problem of husbands and wives living together and facing the new challenges of growing older together. It's clear we need to think of the problem of elder abuse more in the context of spouse abuse. The underlying truth is that an elder is most likely to be abused by the person with whom he or she lives."[4]

The figures show that twice as many elders live with their spouses as with their children. "If more elderly persons lived with their children, there would probably be more child-to-elder violence."[5]

In some cases, a wife or husband will begin abusing an aging or disabled spouse who had been abusive in the past. It is a way to "get back at" the offender. This so-called late-onset spouse abuse, usually by men, is often associated with alcohol or drug abuse, unemployment, postretirement depression, loss of self-esteem, or a history of abuse and violence in the home.

Where children, grandchildren, or closely related family members are guilty of mistreating the elderly, the victim and abuser usually live together, most often in the elder's own home. The arrangement is such that the older person and younger individual are somewhat dependent on each other.

When a parent provides economic support to a dependent, troubled, adult child, there's a higher risk of financial or physical abuse. One thirty-year-old man, for example, had trouble holding down a job and was forced to live at home with his aged parents. He resented his own lack of independence and inability to provide for himself. And he was embarrassed by his financial reliance upon his parents. Unwittingly he turned his resentment into anger. He threatened, intimidated, and harassed the very people on whom he depended. No one even suspected the abuse. In fact, other relatives blamed the old folks for being depressed and crying frequently.

Often the abusers are well-meaning family members who find the home care of an ailing, infirm adult more taxing than they expected. This is especially true when the dependent older person is homebound, incontinent, or the victim of a long-term, behavior-changing illness such as Alzheimer's disease. When caregivers find themselves subject to unusual stress, it can lead to neglect, poor care, or violence.

In one case a seventy-one-year-old man was looking after his mother, who was in her nineties. She kept complaining to neighbors that he was neglecting her. A social worker was sent to investigate. She found that he himself was old and infirm, had had several heart attacks, and was barely able to look after himself.

Adult sons are most frequently named as physical abusers. Usually they are men with a long history of dependence on their mothers, fathers, or other older relatives. In most cases, the physical abuse is accompanied by neglect and psychological abuse. In this so-called transgenerational cycle of violence, the adult child may now be "repaying" the parent for abuse he suffered as a child.

Take the instance of an aged widow who lived in a townhouse in a large city with her fifty-year-old bachelor son. Because the mother had a substantial income, she never pressured her son to work. Since Fred had little to do, he turned to drinking, just like his father. And when Fred got drunk, he beat his mother, just as his father had beat him when he was a child.

Over the years the mother had been treated by doctors five times for fractures and bruises. The son blamed all of these injuries on falls or his mother's "clumsiness." When she was eighty-four, she was hospitalized for fractures of the hip and lower jaw. After the mother came out of the hospital, the son kept her a virtual prisoner in her own home.

The case only came to light when a neighbor told the local priest that the son wouldn't let his mother out of the home. The old woman was removed to a nursing home, where she died shortly afterward. An autopsy revealed evidence of previous beatings and multiple fractures that were caused by her son hitting or pushing her. But without witnesses or additional evidence, no charges could be brought against her son, who continued to live in the home.

Many cases of elder abuse are due to the financial exploitation of both wealthy and not-so-wealthy older persons. One adult daughter in Florida, for example, "helped" her aging mother by managing all of the elderly woman's income—and spending most of it on herself. The son of a seventy-five-year-old man also bilked his father out of his money. When the father became frail following a stroke, his son placed him in a nursing home on public assistance.

THE VICTIMS

Elderly Americans are victims of violent crime less often than those in other age groups. Nevertheless, crimes against the elderly are often more serious and probably more frightening than crimes committed against younger people. Consider the major finding of a recent U.S. Department of Justice report.[6]

Elderly violent crime victims are more likely

to face offenders armed with guns;

to be victimized in or near their own homes;

to offer no resistance during the crime incident

than younger victims.

The rate of injury during a violent attack also rises with age. Thus, violent-crime victims seventy-five and older were more likely to be injured than victims between the ages of sixty-five to seventy-four.[7]

Although there is no clear evidence that one sex is more vulnerable to victimization than the other, elderly men are at greater risk of mistreatment than elderly women. Even though the average male does not live as long as the average female, he is more likely to be dependent on family members. Older women are better able to cope with the loss of a spouse than older men and are more likely to live independently than widowers. In terms of reported victims, older women are probably mentioned more often simply because they survive in greater numbers.

Although men are at greater risk, the typical abuse victim that comes to the attention of authorities is female, with an average age of seventy-five years. She may be ailing, with one or more medical problems. Her money and other possessions may have been stolen, perhaps by relatives. Sometimes her medication, food, and other basic personal needs are denied her. She may be locked in her room, not allowed visitors, and forbidden to make or receive phone calls. At the very least, she may be subjected to a continuing barrage of threats and verbal abuse. At worst, she may be beaten or sexually assaulted.

Pillemer and Finkelhor discovered that elders in poor health are three to four times more likely to be abused than those in good health and that maltreatment cuts across economic, social, religious, and educational lines. They also found that the rates of abuse were no higher for people seventy-five and over than for those sixty-four to seventy-four years old.

Some victims of physical abuse and neglect are incapable—either physically or psychologically—of stopping the abuse. Fear of further punishment or abandonment keeps others quiet. Like abused wives, many victims have a bad self-image and feel they deserve the poor treatment. They may keep telling themselves, "If only I didn't do this, he wouldn't hit me."

But most often the victim keeps quiet because of shame and guilt. "There's a lot of guilt in elder abuse," says Risa Breckman, director of the Elder Abuse Project in the Bronx, New York, "because the family is supposed to be this smiling, happy unit. So a victim thinks, 'How can I tell anyone my son assaulted me? What will they think of our family?' "[8]

Professionals who try to help these victims find that the elderly sometimes refuse to protect themselves from further abuse. Unlike cases of child abuse, which must be reported by law, in some states and in some situations, elder abuse can be kept secret. In other words, the elderly have the legal right to tolerate ill treatment and keep silent if they wish. Controversy can arise, however, when social workers insist on helping the individuals— even if it means having them declared incompetent.

To have someone declared incompetent requires a court order appointing a conservator or a guardian. A conservator is responsible for administering another person's property and assets; a guardian manages both the property and the person. Having a court state that an individual is unable to take care of his or her own affairs can be an absolutely devastating blow. Such action asserts that in the eyes of the law the person is like a child and needs outside control and supervision. Many elderly persons would sooner put up with the abuse than risk such humiliation.

PROTECTION

Abuse of the elderly is a crime regardless of the circumstances. Indeed, there are times when it is necessary to call the cops on an abusing child or family member. Sometimes a legal action—injunction, eviction, or civil commitment—must be taken to get the abuser out of the house and away from the victim.

Forty-four states, including the District of Columbia, have mandatory reporting laws for certain forms of elder abuse that require prosecution. Six others do not.[9]

But the mandatory reporting and other protective-service laws designed to protect the victim do not describe in detail what constitutes criminal abuse of an elderly person. In every state, of course, there are laws on the books forbidding anyone from inflicting physical harm or taking another's money or belongings dishonestly. But is a punch, a slap, or a shove a crime? Is it a crime to neglect someone's needs? Recently, a son in Texas caused his mother to starve to death because he did not provide her with food. During the trial, though, the public prosecutor could not prove that the son purposely tried to kill her, and the son was declared not guilty.[10]

In New York, there is no mandatory-reporting law. A doctor recently became very frustrated when he tried to report a case where an elderly man, who himself was suffering from mental confusion, had severely beaten his wife. She was unwilling to press charges, and no other family members came forward. When the doctor telephoned police, they said they could not get involved in a family affair unless someone filed a formal complaint. A local agency on aging said it lacked legal authority to take action. The woman only got help after she was admitted to the hospital with her injuries and the hospital authorities notified a social service agency.[11]

Where there are statutes that provide for mandatory reporting and intervention, suspected abuse cases come to the attention of a specific city, county, or state agency. But since only about one-fifth of all cases are reported, as many as four out of every five cases remain unknown to the police and social service agencies.

When a report is received, the agency usually investigates within a few days. The investigation, which may involve the police, sometimes uncovers criminal acts or intent, in which case court action can follow.

From time to time, even victims who do speak out find that the system is unable—or unwilling—to respond. A social worker reported an instance in which a seventy-nine-year-old woman asked the court to order her eighty-year-old husband who beat her to stay away from her. The judge, though, thought the matter too impossible to believe and threw the case out of court.[12]

More often, though, cases are handled fairly and justly once they get to court. Not long ago, a neighbor called police to say that a young man had beat his father when the latter refused to give him money. The jury found the son guilty, and he received a five-year prison sentence.[13]

PREVENTION

In 1981 the American Association of Retired Persons (AARP) surveyed 1,001 Americans over age fifty-five and asked them the same question: "If you were a victim of physical abuse, to whom or where would you go for help?" The answers they gave reflected the respondents' considerable confusion and uncertainty:

The police—49 percent.

A friend or relative—17 percent.

My doctor—7 percent.

Don't know—25 percent.[14]

Recently, various organizations have started to develop strategies for communities, families, and individuals to use in the prevention of elder abuse. Among the efforts for communities are support services such as senior daycare centers and "Neighborhood Watch" programs. The latter are set up to organize neighbors to keep a concerned eye on those elderly who have limited social contacts.

Self-help programs have been offered to make it easier for families and individual victims to respond to incidents of mistreatment. Such efforts provide legal advocates for elderly victims. They also deal with any problems that may arise from intervention. For instance, a physically abused elderly woman might be unwilling to sign a complaint against the offender—who could be her child or husband. She also might be unwilling to leave her home—which could also be the home of the abuser. Advocates for the elderly, who are aware of the situation, may work out an arrangement for protecting the victim and for providing housing without completely destroying the family unit.

In recent years, some professionals have suggested that the elderly need help similar to that offered to battered women. "Safe-houses" to go to when afraid of further punishment or consciousness-raising groups to attend for help in facing their problems are two possibilities that have been mentioned. Limited reporting and cutbacks in funds for the elderly would seem to make prevention the best solution to the problem.

The various levels of government and related community agencies are beginning to make an effort to educate the public about elder abuse. They are trying to help individuals establish ways of protecting themselves and lessen the opportunities for abuse. And they are working toward improving the means of intervention should mistreatment occur.

Since alcoholism, drug abuse, and a family history of violence are known indicators of a potential for mistreatment, the presence of these factors can increase the danger to older people. Plans should be made early on, therefore, to remove or reduce the threat. While still reasonably healthy and in command of their faculties, the elderly should decide on living arrangements that will minimize the likelihood of abuse. An elderly widow should not live with an alcoholic son; a frail husband who has been abused by his wife in the past should reside in a setting where there is supervision and help available at all hours.

Physical abuse is rarely the first form of mistreatment. It usually follows a history of emotional or verbal abuse and neglect. If these other forms of mistreatment are recognized early enough, the physical abuse can often be prevented or avoided. Individuals who have been threatened, harassed, humiliated, or neglected need to recognize that these are the warning signs of physical abuse. They can then prepare for intervention or make a change in their living arrangements.

It is, of course, often difficult to predict which situations might trigger abuse. When people cannot recognize their own vulnerability, the family and the community then become responsible.

Family members can prevent mistreatment by recognizing the potential for it and knowing what to do in case of abusive behavior. How can each of us help?

Maintain close ties with aging relatives or friends, especially those who are housebound or otherwise isolated.

Be alert for signs of abuse or neglect.

Become familiar with community services for the aged.

Get to know your older relative's wishes regarding health care in case of incapacitation.

Elderly victims of mistreatment, just like the very young, are the least able to look out for themselves. If all of us help, we may be able to stop this latest form of family violence.

SOURCE NOTES

CHAPTER 1

1. Attorney General's Task Force on Family Violence, Final Report (Washington, DC: U.S. Department of Justice, 1984), p. 11.
2. Patsy A. Klaus and Michael R. Rand, "Family Violence," Bureau of Justice Statistics Special Report (Washington, DC: U.S. Department of Justice, 1989), p. 2.
3. "Battered Women and Criminal Justice: A Report of the Committee on Domestic Violence and Incarcerated Women," June 1987, p. 2.
4. "Koop: Family Violence 'Appalling,' " The Washington COFO Memo, Coalition of Family Organizations, Winter 1987–88, Volume VII, No. 4.
5. Jules Saltman, "The Many Faces of Family Violence" (New York: Public Affairs Pamphlets, No. 640, March 1986), p. 4.
6. Ibid.
7. Ibid., p. 5.
8. Ibid., p. 4.

CHAPTER 2

1. Jules Saltman, "The Many Faces of Family Violence" (New York: Public Affairs Pamphlets, No. 640, March 1986), p. 10.
2. David Finkelhor et al, *The Dark Side of Families: Current Family Violence Research* (Beverly Hills, CA: Sage Publications, 1984), p. 90.
3. Dan Sperling, "Woes of Alcoholics' Daughters," *USA Today*, 2 March 1989, p. A1.
4. Saltman, "Family Violence," p. 10.
5. Martin Daly and Margo Wilson, "Evolutionary Social Psychology and Family Homicide," *Science*, 28 October 1988, pp. 519–24.
6. James Garbarino, *Understanding Abusive Families* (Lexington, MA: D. C. Heath, 1980), p. 32.
7. Richard J. Gelles and Murray A. Straus, *Intimate Violence: The Causes and Consequences of Abuse in the American Family* (New York: Simon and Schuster, 1988), p. 54.
8. Ibid., p. 54.

CHAPTER 3

1. Attorney General's Task Force on Family Violence, Final Report (Washington, DC: U.S. Department of Justice, 1984), p. 11.
2. Ibid., p. 19.
3. Ibid., p. 104.

CHAPTER 4

1. Richard J. Gelles and Murray A. Straus, *Intimate Violence: The Causes and Consequences of Abuse in the American Family* (New York: Simon and Schuster, 1988), p. 61.

2. Michael D. Smith, "Women Abuse in Toronto: Incidence, Prevalence and Demographic Risk Markers," Report No. 18 (Toronto, Canada: York University, 1988), p. 2.
3. Ibid.
4. Ruth A. Brandwein, "Battering Women with Statistics on Violence," *Newsday*, 27 June 1988, p. 51.
5. Murray A. Straus, "Domestic Violence and Homicide Antecedents," *Bulletin of the New York Academy of Medicine*, 62 (1986): 446–65.
6. Brandwein, p. 57.
7. Karen Croke, "He Didn't Hit Me, But . . ." *Daily News*, New York Life section, 22 January 1989, pp. 1, 4.
8. David Finkelhor. *The Dark Side of Families: Current Family Violence Research* (Beverly Hills, CA: Sage Publications, 1984), p. 119.
9. Gelles and Straus, *Intimate Violence*, p. 66.
10. Ibid., p. 67.
11. Susan Brownmiller, "Madly in Love," *Ms.*, April 1989, pp. 56–58.
12. Filomena F. Varvaro, "Domestic Violence," Pamphlet (Pittsburgh, PA: The Women's Center and Shelter of Greater Pittsburgh, 1986).
13. Croke, "He Didn't Hit Me," p. 4.
14. Judy Chicarel, "Offering Hope to Battered Women," *New York Times*, 21 April 1988, p. 18.
15. Ibid.
16. Isabel Wilkerson, "Indianan Uses Prison Furlough to Kill Ex-Wife," *New York Times*, 12 March 1988, p. 22.
17. Rita Henley Jensen, "Battered Women: System Abuse?" *National Law Journal*, 14 December 1987, p. 3.
18. A Report of the Committee on Domestic Violence and Incarcerated Women. "Battered Women and Criminal Justice" (New York: Community Service Society, 1987).

CHAPTER 5

1. Anne H. Cohn, "Physical Abuse." Pamphlet (Chicago, IL: National Committee for the Prevention of Child Abuse), 1989, p. 2.
2. Ibid., p. 3.
3. Timothy Egan, "Child Abuse Cases Draw New Attention," *New York Times.* 1 January 1989, p. A5.
4. Tamar Lewin, "Lisa's Legacy: Awareness of Child Abuse and With It, Alarm," *New York Times*, 1 February 1989, p. B4.
5. Egan, "Child Abuse," p. 5.
6. Cohn, "Physical Abuse," p. 3.
7. Ibid.
8. Richard J. Gelles and Murray A. Straus, *Intimate Violence: The Causes and Consequences of Abuse in the American Family* (New York, Simon and Schuster, 1988), p. 101.
9. Ibid., p. 103.
10. Ibid., p. 135.
11. Donald F. Kline and Anne C. Kline, "The Disabled Child and Child Abuse" (Chicago, IL, The National Committee for the Prevention of Child Abuse, 1987).
12. Gelles and Straus, p. 121.
13. Kline, p. 4.
14. Dena Kleiman, "Stopping Child Abuse Before It Happens," *New York Times*, 6 January 1989, pp. 1, 20.
15. Ibid.

CHAPTER 6

1. C. Everett Koop, "The Surgeon General's Letter on Sexual Abuse" (Washington, DC: Department of Health and Human Services, 1988).
2. John Crewdson, *By Silence Betrayed* (New York: Harper and Row, 1988), p. 27.

3. Jane E. Brody, "Personal Health," *New York Times*, 18 February 1987, Section III, p. 8.
4. David Finkelhor, *Child Sexual Abuse: New Theories and Research* (New York: Free Press, 1984), p. 67.
5. David Finkelhor, "Risk Factors in the Sexual Victimization of Children," *Child Abuse and Neglect* 52 (1980), 265–73.
6. Jon R. Conte, "A Look at Child Sexual Abuse," The National Committee for the Prevention of Child Abuse, 1988.
7. Crewdson, *By Silence Betrayed*, p. 57.
8. Hearing before the Select Committee on Children, Youth and Families, House of Representatives, "Child Abuse and Neglect in America: The Problem and the Response" (Washington, DC: Government Printing Office, 1987).
9. Crewdson, *By Silence Betrayed*, p. 55.
10. Ibid., p. 58.
11. Conte, "Child Sexual Abuse," p. 20.
12. Crewdson, *By Silence Betrayed*, p. 72.
13. Ibid., p. 195.
14. Koop, "Surgeon General's Letter."
15. Anthony Lewis, "Judgment of Solomon." *New York Times*, 15 December 1988, Section I, p. 39.
16. Finkelhor, *Child Sexual Abuse*, p. 84.
17. Crewdson, *By Silence Betrayed*, p. 221.
18. Brody, "Personal Health," p. 8.
19. Crewdson, *By Silence Betrayed*, p. 225.
20. Editorial, "Sex, Cruelty, and Children," *New York Times*, 13 June 1989, p. A26.

CHAPTER 7

1. Ann Wolbert Burgess, "The Sexual Victimization of Adolescents" (Washington, DC: U.S. Department of Health and Human Services, 1985), p. 9.

2. Ibid., p 5.
3. "Sexual Abuse of Children: Selected Readings." National Center on Child Abuse and Neglect, DHHS Publication No. 78-30161, November 1980, p 97.
4. Ibid., p. 4.
5. Burgess, "Adolescents," p 22.
6. Burgess, "Adolescents," p. 19.
7. "Romance and Violence in Dating Relationships." *Journal of Family Issues* (September 1983), 467–82.
8. Robert P. Hall, "Confronting the Issue of Adolescent Sexual Abuse," *News Journal Papers*, 2 July 1987, p. 11.
9. Burgess, "Adolescents," p. 6.
10. Ibid, p. 4.
11. "Romance and Violence. . . ." p. 470.
12. Burgess, "Adolescents," p. 21.
13. William Krasner, "Victims of Rape" (Washington, D.C.: National Institute of Mental Health, 1986), p. 6.
14. Ann Wolbert Burgess, *Sexual Assault of Children and Adolescents* (Lexington, MA: D. C. Heath and Company, 1978), p. 100.
15. Burgess, "Adolescents," pp. 32 and 33.
16. Editorial, "Sex, Cruelty and Children," *New York Times*, 13 June 1989, p. A26.

CHAPTER 8

1. Richard L. Douglass, "Domestic Mistreatment of the Elderly—Towards Prevention" (Washington, DC: Association for the Help of Retired Persons, 1987), p. 17.
2. Karl Pillemer and David Finkelhor, "The Prevalence of Elder Abuse: A Random Sample Survey," University of New Hampshire, Family Violence Research Program, November 1986.
3. "Elders Abused By Their Loved Ones," *USA Today*, September 1987, p. 1.

4. Ibid.
5. Catherine J. Whitaker, "Elderly Victims." Bureau of Justice Statistics, Special Report, U.S. Department of Justice, November 1987.
6. Ibid.
7. Ibid.
8. Elizabeth Holtzman, "The Crime of Parent Abuse," *Newsday*, 3 February 1989, p. 78.
9. Ibid.
10. Annette Winter, "The Shame of Elder Abuse," *Modern Maturity*, October–November 1986, pp. 52–57.
11. Ibid., p. 54.
12. Ibid.
13. Ibid., p. 57.
14. Ibid., p. 54.

BIBLIOGRAPHY

NEWSPAPERS AND MAGAZINES

Modern Maturity
"The Shame of Elder Abuse," October-November, 1986

Ms. magazine
"The Hedda Conundrum," April 1989

Newsday
"Battering Women With Statistics on Violence," 27 June 1988
"The Crime of Parent Abuse," 3 February 1989

Newsweek
"How to Protect Abused Children," 23 November 1987

New York Times
"Family Violence: Protection Improves, but not Prevention," 17 January 1989
"Offering Help to Battered Women," 21 April 1988

"Stopping Child Abuse Before It Happens," 6 January 1989
"Runaways of the 80s: Victims of Abuse," 11 February
1988

Science News
"The Evolution of Family Homicide," 5 November 1988

USA Today
"Woes of Alcoholics' Daughters," 2 March 1989
"Elders Abused By Their Loved Ones," 12 September 1987

PUBLICATIONS

National Committee for the Prevention of Child Abuse.
Physical Child Abuse, 1989
The Disabled Child and Child Abuse, 1987
A Look at Child Sexual Abuse, 1988
Public Affairs Pamphlet No. 640. *The Many Faces of Family
Violence*, March 1986
U.S. Bureau of Justice Statistics Special Report. *Family Vi-
olence*, April 1984
Preventing Domestic Violence Against Women
U.S. Department of Health and Human Services. *The Sex-
ual Victimization of Adolescents*, 1985
The Surgeon General's Letter on Child Sexual Abuse, 1988
Child Abuse and Neglect: A Shared Community Concern,
August 1988
University of New Hampshire. *The Prevalence of Elder Abuse:
A Random Sample Survey*, November 1987

BOOKS

Crewdson, John. *By Silence Betrayed: Sexual Abuse of Children in America*. New York: Harper and Row, 1988.
Gelles, Richard J., and Murray A. Straus, *Intimate Violence: The Causes and Consequences of Abuse in the American Family*. New York: Simon and Schuster, 1988.

Gordon, Linda. *Heroes of Their Own Lives: The Politics and History of Family Violence.* New York: Viking, 1988.

Kaizer, Sherryll. *The Safe Child Book.* New York: Delacorte, 1985.

Kempe, Ruth S., and C. Henry Kempe. *The Common Secret: Sexual Abuse of Children and Adolescents.* San Francisco: W. H. Freeman and Company, 1984.

Straus, Murray, Richard Gelles, and Suzanne Steinmetz. *Behind Closed Doors: Violence in the American Family,* New York: Anchor Books, 1980.

Wachter, Oralee. *No More Secrets For Me.* Boston: Little, Brown, 1984.

INDEX